From Conflict to Unity:

Mastering Church Dynamics

Foreword

This important book by Adam K. Gondwe touches on an issue every church and every Christian ministry will face, whether we admit it or not: conflict will happen even in the most spiritual churches, denominations or ministries. This is due to the fact that while we as Christians have become children of the living God, and while we have received forgiveness for our sins, we still remain sinners.

Adam K. Gondwe in in his book From Conflict to Unity: Mastering Church Dynamics addresses the issue of church politics and of conflict, however, he does not stop their but shows how to handle these kinds of issues in a spiritual and healthy way that will help your Church to blossom.

Gavin Ortlund in his recommendable book Finding the Right Hills to Die On wrote – here especially focusing on the subject of doctrine while his point is certainly also true in a more general way: *"The unity of the church is not an optional add-on – something we can get to later, once we've gotten our doctrine straight. The Church's unity is foundational to her identity and mission."* (page 33)

Adam K. Gondwe speaks exactly to this important issue: How can we maintain (or regain) the unity of our church, our denomination, our ministry? How do we handle church politics or even conflicts? He certainly does not speak from theory, but out of his own experience as a pastor and leader of many years. And you feel this in every chapter. Here is a man who wants to help churches, denominations and ministries to deal with issues in a spiritual way based on biblical principles, as neither our tendencies to avoid or to deny conflicts will help us in any way.

I highly recommend this book to leaders and members of churches, denominations or Christian ministries as it will help you – if you implement the principles offers – to lead your ministry on a spiritual healthy path.

Rev. Prof. Dr. Frank Hinkelmann

Vice Chair of the International Council of the World Evangelical Alliance

Principal of Martin Bucer Seminary, Germany

September 2023

Author's Note:

Thank you for choosing to read **"From Conflict to Unity: Mastering Church Dynamics."** This book comes from my heart, shaped by the many experiences I've had as a pastor and leader. Every church faces its own set of challenges, but I've always believed that with the right guidance, these challenges can be turned into opportunities for growth and unity.

This book is not just about theory; it's about real-life situations that many of us face in ministry. It's about the times when I've had to make tough decisions, handle conflicts, and find ways to bring people together when they seemed worlds apart. I want to share with you what I've learned along the way—lessons that have been hard-earned, but invaluable in helping me lead with wisdom and compassion.

Unity in the church isn't just an ideal—it's essential. It's the foundation that allows us to grow stronger together, to face difficulties with a united front, and to be a true reflection of Christ's love. My hope is that as you read this book, you'll find practical advice that you can apply in your own ministry, but more importantly, I hope you find encouragement and a reminder that you're not alone in this journey.

As you turn these pages, I want you to know that my prayer for you is simple: that you'll be inspired to lead with a heart full of love, a mind full of wisdom, and a spirit ready to embrace the unity that God desires for His church.

May this book be a companion to you as you work to bring your church family closer together, and may it serve as a reminder that with God's guidance, even the toughest challenges can lead to deeper connection and greater strength.

Adam K. Gondwe

From Conflict to Unity:

Mastering Church Dynamics

Table of Contents

From Conflict To Unity

I

Understanding Church Politics

Introduction

Church politics can be a tough and sometimes awkward topic to bring up, but it's so important if we want to build a strong, united community. When we talk about church politics, we're really getting into how power and decisions shape the direction of our church. These things don't just affect how we run programs or make policies—they touch on our spiritual lives and how close we feel as a congregation. By understanding this, we can handle things with care and ensure our church stays a place where everyone grows spiritually and feels connected.

Defining Church Politics

Church politics isn't just about who holds official titles or positions. It's also about the informal ways people influence decisions and shape the church's direction. Whether it's how committees are formed or the subtle ways members advocate for their preferences—whether in church activities or theological ideas—these dynamics have a big impact. Understanding them gives us insight into how things really work behind the scenes and helps us see the full picture of our church's operations.

Importance of Addressing Church Politics

Addressing church politics is essential for several reasons. First, it helps maintain the spiritual health of the congregation. Ignoring these dynamics can lead to mistrust, division, and an unhealthy environment. By recognizing and understanding how power and influence work within the church, we create space for transparency, fairness, and inclusivity—ensuring that everyone feels heard and valued.

Furthermore, effectively navigating church politics can foster greater unity. Understanding the underlying power structures and informal influences allows us to address potential conflicts early, helping to prevent them from escalating. This approach builds an environment where everyone feels a sense of belonging and shared purpose.

The Role of Leadership

Leadership plays a key role in managing church politics. A good leader ensures transparency and inclusion in decisions, making sure that all voices within the church are heard and respected. Leaders who approach issues openly and with fairness help build trust and unity, reducing conflicts and misunderstandings. They are able to guide the congregation through difficult decisions by focusing on respect, fostering a positive environment where everyone feels they have a place and a voice. It's about creating a culture where mutual respect and understanding are at the heart of everything.

Navigating Conflicts

Conflicts are an unavoidable part of any group, and churches are no exception. The way we deal with these challenges can either build up or tear down our congregation. Understanding church politics helps us approach disagreements with wisdom and grace. Instead of letting issues fester, we can address them head-on, getting to the root causes and seeking solutions that bring unity rather than division. When we have a clear understanding of the power dynamics and unspoken influences in our church, we're better equipped to make decisions that benefit everyone.

Handling disputes in this way helps ensure that our church remains a place of love, respect, and spiritual growth for all its members.

Building a Positive Culture

To create a church culture that truly thrives, we need to look beyond the surface and address the underlying dynamics that shape our community. The goal is to foster an environment where the spirit of Christ shines brightly, and where the negative aspects of politics are minimized while the positive elements are elevated.

Imagine a church where humility is not just a concept but a daily practice. Where leaders serve with genuine compassion and members actively support each other's spiritual journeys. This is the kind of environment that reflects Christ's teachings and nurtures true growth.

When humility is at the forefront, we break down barriers and build trust. Service becomes more than a duty—it turns into a way of life that enriches everyone involved. And love? It becomes the heartbeat of our church, guiding our interactions and decisions.

By embracing these values wholeheartedly, we create a community that is not only aligned with the teachings of Christ but also a beacon of support and encouragement. This is where spiritual growth happens organically, and where every member feels valued and uplifted.

Conclusion

Understanding and addressing church politics goes far beyond mere order and control; it's about nurturing a community that thrives on unity and spiritual vitality. Politics in the church isn't just a backdrop to our activities—it's an active force that can either build up or tear down. By digging deep into the dynamics of power and influence, we can transform our church into a place where transparency, fairness, and genuine unity are the norms.

Imagine a church where every member feels heard and valued, where decisions are made openly and with integrity. This kind of environment fosters trust and strengthens our bonds. When we tackle the complexities of church politics with honesty and courage, we pave the way for a more harmonious and spiritually rich community.

Moreover, a church that actively works towards these ideals doesn't just benefit its own members. It stands as a powerful testament to the world of what a Christ-centered community can be. Our efforts to improve transparency and fairness become a shining example of Christian values in action, enhancing our witness to those outside our walls. This, in turn, attracts others who are searching for a place where faith and integrity truly intersect.

II

Dynamics of Power and Influence

In every organization, including churches, the interplay of power and influence is crucial in shaping decisions and guiding leadership. For churches, these dynamics are even more pivotal because they impact not just the daily operations but also the spiritual journey and overall health of the community.

This chapter delves into the intricate structures of power within churches, examining the roles and responsibilities of leaders and how influence plays a role in decision-making. Understanding these aspects helps us see the broader picture of how churches operate and how both members and leaders can collaborate effectively.

By exploring these dynamics, we uncover valuable insights into fostering a thriving faith community. It's about creating a space where leadership is not only effective but also aligned with spiritual values, and where every member feels engaged and valued. This approach not only enhances the internal life of the church but also strengthens its mission and impact in the wider world.

Power Structures in Churches

Power structures play a significant role in guiding how the church operates and who holds authority. These structures may seem rigid at times, but they are essential for maintaining order and ensuring that the church functions effectively. For instance, a typical church might have a senior pastor who provides overall spiritual direction, associate pastors who manage specific ministries, deacons who support the pastors, and various committees that focus on areas like finance, outreach, and education.

The Apostle Paul reminds us of the importance of order within the church when he writes in *1 Corinthians 14:40, "Let all things be done decently and in order."* Understanding these power structures helps us recognize who makes important decisions and the rationale behind them. In some churches, decision-making power may be concentrated among a few leaders at the top. In others, power may be more distributed, with significant input from the congregation through meetings and votes. Regardless of the setup, it is crucial to comprehend how these structures work for anyone wishing to get involved or understand the church's internal workings.

Leadership Roles and Their Implications

Leadership in the church isn't just about the spotlight on Sundays; it's a full-time commitment with many layers. Think about the senior pastor. They're not only up there delivering inspiring sermons but are also the heartbeat of the church's vision. They provide pastoral care, offering a listening ear and guidance to those in need, and juggle a myriad of administrative tasks to keep everything running smoothly.

Then there are the associate pastors and ministry leaders. Their roles might not always be in the limelight, but they're just as crucial. Whether it's organizing youth events that spark enthusiasm in young hearts or leading worship services that bring everyone together in song, their efforts are the backbone of a vibrant church community.

Each role, big or small, contributes to the church's mission in unique ways. Recognizing the depth and dedication of these roles helps us appreciate the hard work that goes into creating a nurturing and dynamic faith community. By understanding and supporting each other's roles, we build a stronger, more connected church family.

The Bible emphasizes the gravity of leadership with passages such as *James 3:1, "My brethren, be not many masters, knowing that we shall receive the greater condemnation."* This verse underscores the weight of leadership and the need for wisdom and integrity. Church leaders must wield their influence with humility and prioritize the needs of the congregation. Leaders who misuse their power can cause division and mistrust. Therefore, it is essential for leaders to remain grounded in their role as servants, as Jesus demonstrated in *Mark 10:45: "For even the Son of man came not to be ministered unto, but to minister, and to give his life a ransom for many."*

Influence and Decision-Making

Influence in a church isn't just about who holds official titles. It's often found in unexpected places. For instance, think of the long-time member who's been around for years—they might not be on the leadership team, but their deep connections and wisdom make them a guiding light for many. Or consider the charismatic volunteer who has a natural way of inspiring others and rallying them around new initiatives. And let's not forget the person with a profound grasp of the Bible, who, though they might not lead a ministry, offers invaluable guidance and insight to those seeking spiritual growth.

These individuals, each in their own way, play a significant role in shaping the church community. Their influence helps build the church's culture and drives its mission forward, proving that everyone has something important to contribute. Recognizing and valuing this broad spectrum of influence enriches our understanding of how the church truly functions and grows.

Decision-making in churches often involves a blend of formal and informal processes. Some decisions are made through official meetings and votes, while others may be shaped by informal discussions and the opinions of influential members. *Proverbs 15:22* states, *"Without counsel purposes are disappointed: but in the multitude of counsellors they are established."* This verse highlights the value of seeking diverse perspectives in decision-making. The factors influencing decisions can range from church traditions and values to the personal preferences of leaders and the needs of the congregation.

The Importance of Transparency

Transparency is crucial for maintaining healthy power dynamics in a church. When leaders are upfront about how decisions are made and why certain choices are being taken, it fosters a sense of trust and strengthens the community. It's like shining a light on the process, so everyone can see how things work and why they're happening the way they are.

For example, sharing meeting minutes keeps everyone in the loop about what's being discussed and decided. Holding open forums allows members to voice their thoughts and ask questions, making them feel more involved and heard. Being honest about challenges and decisions, even when it's tough, shows respect and builds a stronger, more cohesive community.

By prioritizing transparency, we can prevent rumors and misunderstandings from taking root, making everyone feel valued and engaged in the church's journey. It's about creating an environment where trust and openness are the norm, enhancing our collective spirit and mission.

Proverbs 12:19 states, *"The lip of truth shall be established for ever: but a lying tongue is but for a moment."* This verse underscores the importance of honesty and openness. Leaders should strive to create an environment where transparency is a priority, as this encourages trust and unity among members.

Encouraging Healthy Influence

Healthy influence in a church isn't just about formal roles or titles—it's about the genuine connection between people, built on respect, collaboration, and humility. When everyone feels their voice is truly valued, it strengthens the entire church community.

Leaders can make this happen by actively listening to different viewpoints, being approachable, and welcoming feedback with an open heart. Imagine regular town hall meetings where members can speak up, ask questions, and share their ideas. These gatherings make everyone feel more involved and part of something bigger.

By creating a space where respect and collaboration are at the core, leaders and members together build a church where everyone feels connected and engaged. It's about making sure everyone has a place and a voice in shaping the community's journey.

Philippians 2:3 encourages us to adopt a mindset of humility: *"Let nothing be done through strife or vainglory; but in lowliness of mind let each esteem other better than themselves."* By embracing this attitude, we create a more inclusive and supportive environment where healthy influence thrives.

Conclusion

Power and influence are part of every community, and the church is no different. But when we truly understand these dynamics and focus on being transparent and inclusive, we create a space where everyone feels seen and valued.

Imagine a church where open conversations are encouraged, and every member feels like they have a say. This kind of environment not only strengthens our connections with each other but also makes us more effective in our mission to serve and share our message with the world.

By approaching these dynamics with wisdom and a genuine spirit of love, we help each other grow in faith and ensure that our church moves forward with a clear sense of unity and purpose. It's all about making sure every voice is heard, and every person feels like they're an important part of the journey.

III

Navigating Conflicts and Disagreements

Conflict is a natural part of life, and churches aren't immune. Just like any community, a church brings together people with different backgrounds, perspectives, and personalities. While these differences can add richness to our shared experiences, they can also spark misunderstandings and disagreements.

But here's the thing: when we approach conflicts with thoughtfulness and a biblical perspective, they can actually bring us closer together. Tackling issues head-on and resolving them with grace and wisdom helps build a stronger, more united church community. It's about turning challenges into opportunities for growth and deepening our connections with one another. In the end, handling conflicts well not only resolves the immediate issues but also strengthens the bonds that hold us together.

As believers, we are called to maintain the unity of the Spirit in the bond of peace. *"Endeavour to keep the unity of the Spirit in the bond of peace."* (Ephesians 4:3) This endeavor requires effort, patience, and a deep reliance on God's guidance. Conflicts, when handled in a Christ-like manner, can be opportunities for growth and deeper relationships within the church.

<u>Types of Conflicts</u>

Understanding where conflicts often come from can really help us handle them better and keep the peace in our congregation. By recognizing the typical sources of tension—whether it's differences in opinion, communication breakdowns, or unmet expectations—we can tackle these issues more effectively. This awareness allows us to address problems early and work towards solutions that keep our community harmonious and strong.

Theological Differences

One of the most profound sources of conflict within a church can be disagreements over doctrine or the interpretation of the Bible. Such conflicts can emerge between different denominations or even within the same congregation, especially when new teachings or perspectives challenge traditional beliefs. For example, introducing contemporary worship practices in a traditionally conservative church can cause tension among members who feel their long-held traditions are being compromised. The Apostle Paul warned of such divisions, urging believers to *"speak the same thing, and that there be no divisions among you; but that ye be perfectly joined together in the same mind and in the same judgment."* (1 Corinthians 1:10)

Leadership Disputes

Conflicts can also arise from power struggles or disagreements on leadership styles. This might involve disputes over decision-making processes, changes in church direction, or personal differences among leaders. Leadership conflicts can become particularly contentious when there is a lack of clear communication or when leaders fail to seek consensus on important decisions. *"Obey them that have the rule over you, and submit yourselves: for they watch for your souls, as they that must give account."* (Hebrews 13:17) This verse underscores the importance of respecting church leadership while also reminding leaders of their responsibility to shepherd the congregation with care and humility.

Personal Conflicts

Personal conflicts between church members are perhaps the most common. These can stem from misunderstandings, personality clashes, or offenses that have not been addressed. In a close-knit community, even minor issues can escalate if not resolved promptly. Jesus taught us in *"Moreover if thy brother shall trespass against thee, go and tell him his fault between thee and him alone: if he shall hear thee, thou hast gained thy brother."* (Matthew 18:15) This highlights the importance of addressing personal grievances directly and privately to prevent them from growing into larger conflicts.

Generational Gaps

Differences between age groups can also lead to misunderstandings and conflicts. Younger members may desire change and modernization, while older members might prefer tradition and stability. Bridging this gap requires mutual respect and understanding. *"Let no man despise thy youth; but be thou an example of the believers, in word, in conversation, in charity, in spirit, in faith, in purity."* (1 Timothy 4:12) Encourages younger members to lead by example, while older members are reminded to value their contributions.

Conflict Resolution

Addressing conflicts with grace and wisdom involves applying biblical principles and practical strategies. Here are some key approaches:

Seek God's Guidance

Prayer is essential in resolving conflicts. Ask God for wisdom, patience, and a heart that seeks reconciliation. *"If any of you lack wisdom, let him ask of God, that giveth to all men liberally, and upbraideth not; and it shall be given him."* (James 1:5) Seeking God's guidance ensures that our actions and decisions are aligned with His will.

Open Communication

Effective communication is vital in conflict resolution. Ensure that all parties involved have an opportunity to express their views and feelings without interruption. Listen actively and empathetically. *"Wherefore, my beloved brethren, let every man be swift to hear, slow to speak, slow to wrath."* (James 1:19) This verse reminds us of the importance of listening before reacting.

Mediation

Sometimes, conflicts may require the intervention of a neutral third party to mediate and help find a resolution.

This can be a church leader or an external mediator who is trusted and respected by all parties. *"Blessed are the peacemakers: for they shall be called the children of God."* (Matthew 5:9) Peacemakers play a crucial role in facilitating reconciliation and healing.

Forgiveness and Reconciliation

Forgiveness is a cornerstone of Christian conflict resolution. Holding onto grudges only deepens divisions. Jesus emphasized the importance of forgiveness in *"For if ye forgive men their trespasses, your heavenly Father will also forgive you: But if ye forgive not men their trespasses, neither will your Father forgive your trespasses."* (Matthew 6:14-15) Embracing forgiveness paves the way for genuine reconciliation.

Focus on Unity

Remember the ultimate goal of conflict resolution is to restore unity and peace within the church. *"Behold, how good and how pleasant it is for brethren to dwell together in unity!"* (Psalm 133:1) Unity is a testament to the world of God's love and the transformative power of the Gospel.

Understanding the different types of conflicts that can pop up in a church and using biblical principles to address them can help us handle disagreements in a way that honors God and brings us closer together. The road to resolution might be tough at times, but with prayer, humility, and a genuine desire for peace, we can work through conflicts and create a more unified and loving church family. It's about tackling issues with a heart for healing and focusing on strengthening our bonds with one another.

Implementing a Conflict Resolution Strategy

To effectively resolve conflicts and promote harmony, it is crucial to implement a structured approach that aligns with biblical principles and practical strategies. Here's a comprehensive guide to navigating conflicts within the church:

Establish Clear Procedures

Having clear procedures for handling disputes can help manage conflicts more effectively. This might involve setting up a church committee dedicated to conflict resolution or outlining steps in the church's bylaws for addressing grievances. *"Let all things be done decently and in order."* (1 Corinthians 14:40) Establishing order and clarity ensures that conflicts are handled in a fair and systematic manner.

Encourage Accountability

Encourage church members to take responsibility for their actions and words. Accountability helps prevent conflicts from escalating and promotes a culture of honesty and integrity. *"Confess your faults one to another, and pray one for another, that ye may be healed."* (James 5:16) This verse highlights the importance of acknowledging mistakes and seeking forgiveness.

Promote Empathy and Understanding

Fostering a culture of empathy within the church can help prevent conflicts and ease tensions when they arise. Encourage members to consider others' perspectives and experiences. *"Rejoice with them that do rejoice, and weep with them that weep."* (Romans 12:15) Empathy builds stronger relationships and helps to bridge gaps between differing viewpoints.

Educate on Conflict Resolution

Providing training or workshops on conflict resolution can equip church members with the skills they need to handle disagreements constructively. This might include teaching active listening, negotiation techniques, and biblical conflict resolution principles. *"The heart of the prudent getteth knowledge; and the ear of the wise seeketh knowledge."* (Proverbs 18:15) Education empowers individuals to handle conflicts with wisdom and understanding.

Foster a Culture of Forgiveness

Promoting forgiveness as a core value of the church helps to create a more supportive and loving environment. Encourage members to forgive one another just as Christ forgave us. *"And be ye kind one to another, tenderhearted, forgiving one another, even as God for Christ's sake hath forgiven you."* (Ephesians 4:32) Emphasizing forgiveness leads to healing and reconciliation.

Evaluate and Reflect

After a conflict has been resolved, take time to evaluate the process and reflect on what was learned. This can help prevent similar issues in the future and improve conflict resolution strategies. *"The way of a fool is right in his own eyes: but he that hearkeneth unto counsel is wise."* (Proverbs 12:15) Reflection and counsel lead to growth and better practices.

Conclusion

Navigating conflicts within a church takes a thoughtful mix of biblical wisdom and practical steps. It's all about understanding the kinds of conflicts that can pop up and knowing how to handle them effectively to keep our church community strong and loving.

Conflicts are a part of life, but they don't have to tear us apart. When we approach them with grace and understanding, and use biblical principles to guide us, we turn potential problems into chances for growth and deeper connections. Remember what Christ said: *"Blessed are the peacemakers: for they shall be called the children of God"* (Matthew 5:9). By being peacemakers, we embody the love and grace of our Lord, and create a church environment where every member feels valued and united.

IV

Leadership and Integrity

In the realm of church leadership, the role is as broad as it is deep. Leaders not only guide their congregations spiritually but also juggle the day-to-day operations of the church. It's a rewarding yet challenging position that demands a delicate balance between spiritual insight and practical management.

Imagine the weight of this dual responsibility: inspiring faith while also making sure the church runs smoothly. Leaders face the task of making ethical decisions and upholding personal integrity, all while staying true to biblical principles. It's about being transparent and honest, even when faced with tough choices.

Understanding these challenges reveals that a church's strength lies in its leaders' ability to navigate their roles with wisdom and faithfulness. It's this blend of spiritual guidance and practical know-how that truly supports and enriches the entire church community.

Leadership Challenges

Leading a church isn't just about guiding spiritual growth; it's also about managing a complex organization. This dual role comes with its own set of challenges, especially when it comes to balancing ethical considerations with practical needs.

Leaders must navigate the delicate dance of providing spiritual direction while ensuring that the church operates efficiently and responsibly. It's about making decisions that honor both the spiritual mission of the church and the practical demands of running an organization. This balancing act can be tough, but it's crucial for creating a thriving and harmonious church community.

Ethical Dilemmas:

Church leaders often encounter ethical dilemmas that test their moral fortitude and decision-making skills. These issues can range from handling financial resources responsibly to managing personal conflicts of interest. For instance, a leader might face the temptation to misuse church funds for personal gain or to avoid addressing problematic behaviors within the congregation to maintain peace. Such dilemmas require a steadfast commitment to biblical values. *"The just man walketh in his integrity: his children are blessed after him."* (Proverbs 20:7) Integrity in leadership involves making decisions that align with God's principles, even when it's difficult or unpopular.

Spiritual Leadership vs. Organizational Management:

Church leaders must juggle the roles of spiritual guide and organizational manager. This balancing act involves making decisions that affect both the spiritual and operational aspects of the church. Leaders must address practical concerns such as budgeting, staffing, and compliance with legal regulations while maintaining a focus on spiritual growth and mission. *"Moreover it is required in stewards, that a man be found faithful."* (1 Corinthians 4:2) Faithfulness means being reliable and consistent in both spiritual and managerial duties, ensuring that all actions are taken with integrity and commitment to the church's mission.

Navigating Tensions:

Leaders often face situations where the best course of action for the church's spiritual health may conflict with organizational or practical needs. For example, a decision to address a financial shortfall might involve difficult conversations or unpopular changes that affect the congregation. Leaders must seek God's guidance and rely on prayer, wise counsel, and a commitment to fairness to navigate these tensions. *"If any of you lack wisdom, let him ask of God, that giveth to all men liberally, and upbraideth not; and it shall be given him."* (James 1:5) Seeking divine wisdom helps leaders make balanced decisions that honor both spiritual and practical considerations.

Cultivating Integrity

Maintaining integrity is crucial for leaders to build trust and credibility within their congregation. Integrity means being transparent, accountable, and consistent in one's morals. It's about ensuring that leaders' actions align with their teachings and values. When leaders act with integrity, they not only earn respect but also inspire confidence and commitment within their community. This alignment between words and actions fosters a deeper sense of trust and strengthens the overall unity of the church.

Transparency:

Transparency involves being open and honest about decisions, processes, and actions, particularly concerning sensitive areas such as finances and governance. Leaders should communicate clearly with the congregation about how resources are managed and how decisions are made. *"But let your communication be, Yea, yea; Nay, nay: for whatsoever is more than these cometh of evil."* (Matthew 5:37) Clear and honest communication helps prevent misunderstandings and fosters a culture of trust within the church.

Accountability:

Accountability means being responsible for one's actions and decisions. Effective leaders establish mechanisms for oversight, such as boards or committees, to provide checks and balances. This process helps ensure that leaders are held accountable for their actions and that decisions are made in the best interest of the church. *"A fool uttereth all his mind: but a wise man keepeth it in till afterwards."* (Proverbs 29:11) Accountability encourages careful consideration of actions and fosters a culture of responsibility and trust.

Moral Integrity:

Moral integrity requires leaders to uphold high ethical standards and live in accordance with biblical principles. This involves not only personal conduct but also ensuring that church policies and practices reflect these standards. *"But the fruit of the Spirit is love, joy, peace, longsuffering, gentleness, goodness, faith, Meekness, temperance: against such there is no law."* (Galatians 5:22-23) Leaders who embody the fruits of the Spirit demonstrate moral integrity and set an example for others to follow.

Practical Strategies for Cultivating Integrity:

1. **Regular Reflection and Prayer:** Leaders should engage in regular personal reflection and prayer to seek

guidance and maintain alignment with God's will. This practice helps leaders stay grounded in their values and makes it easier to navigate complex decisions. *"The integrity of the upright shall guide them: but the perverseness of transgressors shall destroy them."* (Proverbs 11:3) Regular reflection and prayer ensure that leaders remain steadfast in their commitment to integrity.

2. **Seek Accountability Partners:** Establishing relationships with trusted individuals who can provide advice, support, and accountability is crucial. These partners can offer objective perspectives and help leaders stay true to their values. *"Iron sharpeneth iron; so a man sharpeneth the countenance of his friend."* (Proverbs 27:17) Accountability partners play a vital role in maintaining integrity and ensuring that leaders remain focused on their mission.

3. **Establish Clear Policies and Procedures:** Implementing clear policies and procedures for church operations helps ensure consistency and transparency. These policies should cover financial management, conflict resolution, and decision-making processes. *"Let all things be done decently and in order."* (1 Corinthians 14:40) Well-defined policies provide a framework for ethical conduct and help leaders make informed decisions.

4. **Model Integrity:** Leaders should lead by example, demonstrating integrity in all aspects of their lives. When leaders model ethical behavior, they set a standard for the congregation to follow. *"Be thou an example of the believers, in word, in conversation, in*

charity, in spirit, in faith, in purity." (1 Timothy 4:12) By embodying their values, leaders inspire others to live with integrity and uphold the same standards.

Conclusion

Leadership within the church involves navigating the delicate balance between spiritual guidance and practical management. Addressing ethical dilemmas with wisdom and maintaining integrity through transparency, accountability, and moral steadfastness is essential for effective leadership. By emphasizing these principles, leaders build trust, foster a positive environment, and strengthen the church community. As leaders strive to embody these qualities, they reflect the teachings of Christ and promote a spirit of unity and righteousness within the church.

V

Building Unity Amidst Diversity

Embracing Diversity as a Strength

In the life of a church, diversity is a natural and invaluable aspect that can greatly enrich the community. The church is made up of people from different backgrounds, cultures, and experiences, each bringing their own unique perspective to the collective worship and fellowship. This diversity—whether theological, cultural, or generational—is not something to be managed or minimized but celebrated and cherished.

The Bible clearly demonstrates that diversity is an integral part of God's creation. In *Revelation 7:9*, it is written, *"After this I beheld, and, lo, a great multitude, which no man could number, of all nations, and kindreds, and people, and tongues, stood before the throne, and before the Lamb, clothed with white robes, and palms in their hands."* This vision of heaven shows a diverse multitude unified in worship before God. It reminds us that diversity reflects the grandeur of God's creation and His inclusive love.

Embracing and celebrating diversity within the church creates a richer, more vibrant community. Imagine a church that welcomes different cultural traditions—it opens the door to a wider array of worship styles, musical expressions, and communal practices. This diversity not only adds depth to the church's spiritual life but also brings unique insights and practices that can enrich everyone's faith journey.

When different cultures and traditions come together, they create a tapestry of worship that reflects the fullness of God's creation. This variety can deepen the collective faith experience, making it more inclusive and dynamic. It's about appreciating and learning from each other's backgrounds, which ultimately strengthens and enhances the entire church community.

Theological diversity is another aspect to celebrate. Different interpretations and understandings of Scripture can lead to a more comprehensive view of God's truth. This variety of perspectives encourages deeper study and discussion, which can lead to greater spiritual growth and unity in understanding. As Paul writes in *1 Corinthians 12:14, "For the body is not one member, but many."* Each person's unique theological perspective contributes to the overall health of the church body.

Generational diversity also plays a crucial role in the church. Older generations offer wisdom and experience, while younger generations bring energy and new ideas. This interplay can foster a dynamic environment where all ages learn from and support each other. It echoes the sentiment of *Psalm 145:4, "One generation shall praise thy works to another, and shall declare thy mighty acts."* This mutual exchange of knowledge and experience strengthens the church community and helps bridge gaps between different age groups.

Promoting Unity Amidst Differences

While diversity is a strength, it can also present challenges. Different opinions, traditions, and practices can sometimes lead to misunderstandings or conflicts. Therefore, promoting unity within a diverse church community is essential for maintaining harmony and effectiveness.

One effective strategy for fostering unity is to emphasize common values and goals. By focusing on the shared mission and purpose of the church, members can find common ground even amidst differing opinions. *Philippians 2:2* encourages this approach: *"Fulfil ye my joy, that ye be like-minded, having the same love, being of one accord, of one mind."* When members align themselves with the church's overarching vision, it becomes easier to navigate through disagreements and work together towards common objectives.

Creating a culture of respect and understanding is also vital for promoting unity. Encouraging open dialogue and actively listening to others can help bridge gaps between differing viewpoints. The Proverbs remind us of the importance of listening: *"He that answereth a matter before he heareth it, it is folly and shame unto him" (Proverbs 18:13)*. This approach fosters an environment where every voice is heard and valued, reducing the likelihood of misunderstandings and building stronger connections among members.

Church leaders play a crucial role in modeling unity. Their behavior and attitudes set the tone for how conflicts and differences are addressed within the congregation. Leaders who practice humility, patience, and fairness can guide their communities towards greater harmony. *Ephesians 4:2-3* instructs us, *"With all lowliness and meekness, with long-suffering, forbearing one another in love; Endeavouring to keep the unity of the Spirit in the bond of peace."* Leaders who embody these qualities help create an environment where unity is actively pursued and maintained.

Moreover, recognizing and celebrating each person's contributions can help promote a sense of belonging and unity. By affirming the unique gifts and talents of each member, the church strengthens its community bonds. *Romans 12:4-5* illustrates this concept: *"For as we have many members in one body, and all members have not the same office: So we, being many, are one body in Christ, and every one members one of another."* Valuing each person's role within the church reinforces the idea that every contribution is important, and that diversity enriches the body of Christ.

Conclusion

Building unity in the midst of diversity takes intentional effort and a genuine commitment to embracing our differences. It starts with focusing on the common values that bind us together, encouraging respectful dialogue, and leading by example to model the unity we seek.

When a church actively celebrates its diversity while striving for unity, it creates a vibrant community where everyone feels valued and included. This approach not only strengthens our internal connections but also boosts our ability to carry out our mission effectively.

Let's approach our diverse community with love, humility, and grace, always aiming to uplift one another in faith and unity. By doing so, we foster a church environment where diversity enriches our collective experience and unity becomes a powerful testament to our shared purpose.

VI

Spiritual Health and Discernment

Navigating the complexities of church life goes beyond just having strong organizational skills and strategic planning; it requires a deep, abiding connection with God. Spiritual health and discernment are at the heart of leading a meaningful and impactful Christian life.

As church leaders and members, we are called to cultivate a discerning spirit to make wise decisions, protect our spiritual well-being, and stay aligned with God's will. This chapter will delve into how we can nurture discernment and safeguard our spiritual health amid the demands of church life. We'll explore biblical principles and practices designed to keep us grounded in our faith, ensuring that our journey remains anchored in God's guidance and love.

Nurturing a Discerning Spirit

Spiritual discernment is key to making wise decisions and understanding God's will in different situations. It's about seeking God's guidance through prayer, immersing ourselves in Scripture, and being attuned to the Holy Spirit's leading. This process allows us to look beyond our immediate circumstances and grasp the deeper significance of our choices. By tuning into this divine guidance, we gain clarity and insight, helping us navigate life's complexities with a sense of purpose and alignment with God's plan.

The Bible promises that God will give wisdom to those who seek it. *James 1:5* assures us, *"If any of you lack wisdom, let him ask of God, that giveth to all men liberally, and upbraideth not; and it shall be given him."* This promise encourages us to actively seek God's wisdom in all aspects of our lives, including decisions related to church matters.

To cultivate a discerning spirit, it is crucial to develop a close relationship with God. This relationship is fostered through consistent prayer and meditation. *1 Thessalonians 5:17* instructs us to *"Pray without ceasing."* Regular communication with God helps us to stay aligned with His will and gain clarity on complex issues.

Discernment also involves understanding and applying biblical principles to our decisions. *Proverbs 3:5-6* advises us to *"Trust in the Lord with all thine heart; and lean not unto thine own understanding. In all thy ways acknowledge him, and he shall direct thy paths."* By trusting in God and seeking His guidance, we align our decisions with His purposes and maintain a clear sense of direction.

Humility is a key component of discernment. Recognizing our limitations and being open to God's direction helps us approach decisions with a humble heart. *1 Peter 5:5* reminds us to *"be clothed with humility: for God resisteth the proud, and giveth grace to the humble."* This humility allows us to listen to others, consider different perspectives, and make decisions that honor God and serve the community.

Guarding Spiritual Health

Staying spiritually healthy is crucial for keeping our faith strong and handling the ups and downs of church life. It's not just about showing up on Sundays; it's about really nurturing our relationship with God and diving into practices that keep our faith alive and vibrant.

This means making time for daily prayer, diving into the Bible, and connecting with a supportive community of fellow believers. It also involves taking moments for personal reflection and spiritual refreshment. By weaving these practices into our daily lives, we keep our spiritual health in check and find the strength and clarity to face life's challenges with a deeper sense of purpose.

One essential practice for guarding spiritual health is regular prayer. Prayer is our primary means of communication with God and helps us stay connected with Him. *Philippians 4:6* encourages us to *"be careful for nothing; but in every thing by prayer and supplication with thanksgiving let your requests be made known unto God."* Through prayer, we find peace, guidance, and strength.

Engaging with Scripture is another crucial practice for spiritual vitality. The Bible provides wisdom, encouragement, and guidance. *Psalm 119:105* says, *"Thy word is a lamp unto my feet, and a light unto my path."* Regularly reading and reflecting on God's Word helps us grow in faith and understanding, guiding us through life's challenges.

Participation in Christian fellowship also supports spiritual health. Being part of a supportive and nurturing community offers encouragement, accountability, and opportunities for growth. *Hebrews 10:24-25* emphasizes the importance of fellowship: *"And let us consider one another to provoke unto love and to good works: Not forsaking the assembling of ourselves together, as the manner of some is; but exhorting one another: and so much the more, as ye see the day approaching."* Fellowship strengthens our faith and helps us remain connected with others in the body of Christ.

Additionally, engaging in spiritual disciplines such as fasting, worship, and service plays a significant role in maintaining spiritual vitality. These practices help us focus on God, develop self-discipline, and contribute to the well-being of others. *Matthew 6:16-18* addresses fasting: *"Moreover when ye fast, be not, as the hypocrites, of a sad countenance: for they disfigure their faces, that they may appear unto men to fast. Verily I say unto you, They have their reward. But thou, when thou fastest, anoint thine head, and wash thy face; That thou appear not unto men to fast, but unto thy Father which is in secret: and thy Father, which seeth in secret, shall reward thee openly."* This passage highlights the importance of sincerity and personal commitment in our spiritual practices.

Conclusion

Spiritual discernment and health are crucial for living a vibrant Christian life. When we nurture a discerning spirit, we're better equipped to make decisions that align with God's will. At the same time, keeping our spiritual health in check helps us stay strong and resilient through the challenges that come with church life.

By committing to practices like prayer, engaging with Scripture, participating in fellowship, and embracing spiritual disciplines, we build a robust and dynamic faith. Approaching these practices with sincerity and dedication allows us to navigate our spiritual journey with clarity, purpose, and a deep connection to God. This helps us face life's challenges with a steady heart and a clear sense of direction.

VII

Transparency and Communication

In any church, transparency is the bedrock of trust, unity, and smooth operations. When leaders and members are open about their actions, decisions, and processes, it fosters a sense of inclusion and respect. Transparency goes beyond just sharing information; it means ensuring that everything from planning and strategy to finances and daily operations is handled with honesty and clarity.

This chapter will dive into why transparency matters so much and offer practical tips for making it a reality in every aspect of church life. By embracing transparency, we build a community where everyone feels informed, valued, and truly part of the journey.

Importance of Transparency

Transparency isn't just a buzzword; it's a vital value that touches every part of church life. It means that members are kept in the loop about how decisions are made and how resources are allocated, which builds trust and a sense of belonging.

When a church operates with transparency, it helps prevent misunderstandings and reduces conflicts, making the ministry more effective overall. This openness encourages honest conversations and meaningful involvement, which are key to fostering a healthy and vibrant church community. By embracing transparency, we create an environment where everyone feels informed, included, and empowered to contribute to the church's mission.

Proverbs 12:22 tells us, *"Lying lips are abomination to the Lord: but they that deal truly are his delight."* This verse highlights the importance of honesty and truthfulness in all our dealings, including within the church. Being transparent aligns with these biblical principles and demonstrates a commitment to integrity.

Transparency in Planning

Effective planning is key to making any church initiative or program successful. When planning is done openly, everyone involved knows the goals, processes, and expected results. This transparency not only keeps everyone informed but also encourages members to pitch in their ideas and feedback.

When people are part of the planning process, it makes the plans feel more connected to the whole congregation's vision. This way, everyone feels a sense of ownership and commitment, which boosts the chances of success and ensures the initiative truly resonates with the community.

The Bible supports the value of thorough planning and openness. *Proverbs 15:22* states, *"Without counsel purposes are disappointed: but in the multitude of counsellors they are established."* Involving various members in the planning process not only helps in making well-informed decisions but also builds a sense of ownership and commitment to the church's goals.

To ensure transparency in planning, leaders can hold regular strategy sessions where they openly discuss plans with key stakeholders. By sharing detailed documentation of these plans and decisions, and making them accessible to the entire congregation, leaders help everyone stay informed and aligned with the church's mission and values. This approach not only fosters trust but also ensures that everyone feels included and up to date with the church's direction.

Transparency in Strategy

Strategic decisions play a crucial role in shaping the direction and growth of a church. Transparency in this area means being clear about the church's long-term goals, the reasons behind major decisions, and the methods used to achieve them.

When leaders openly share their strategic choices, it helps members grasp the church's vision and understand how their efforts fit into the bigger picture. This openness not only fosters a sense of involvement but also encourages everyone to work together toward common goals, creating a united and motivated community.

Luke 14:28 highlights the importance of planning and strategy: *"For which of you, intending to build a tower, sitteth not down first, and counteth the cost, whether he have sufficient to finish it?"* This verse emphasizes the need for careful planning and open discussion about the resources and efforts required to achieve strategic goals.

Keeping everyone updated on strategic initiatives and involving members in discussions about the church's future is essential for staying on track and making sure our plans are effective. Leaders should share the reasons behind big decisions and actively seek feedback from the congregation. This way, everyone feels included and connected to the church's mission.

When we approach planning as a team, it strengthens our sense of unity and shared purpose, making us all more invested in achieving our goals together. By being open and collaborative, we build a church community that's not only engaged but excited about our journey forward.

Transparency in Finances

Financial transparency is key to building trust and accountability within the church. Members deserve to know how their contributions are being used and how financial decisions are made.

Transparent financial practices mean regularly sharing updates on income and expenses, clearly explaining budgetary choices, and having open discussions about financial needs and goals. When we keep finances open and accessible, we not only uphold trust but also foster a sense of partnership and shared responsibility in the church's mission.

The Bible provides guidance on financial integrity. *1 Timothy 5:18* says, *"For the scripture saith, Thou shalt not muzzle the ox that treadeth out the corn. And, The labourer is worthy of his reward."* This verse underscores the principle that those who contribute to the church's work should be fairly compensated and that financial matters should be handled with honesty and fairness.

To promote financial transparency, churches should regularly share detailed financial reports with the congregation, covering income, expenditures, and budget forecasts. Holding financial workshops or meetings where members can ask questions and give feedback helps create an environment of openness and trust. This approach ensures that everyone is informed about how funds are managed and encourages active participation in the church's financial well-being.

Transparency in Operations

Daily operations include all the everyday tasks that keep the church running smoothly. Being transparent in these operations means being open about how decisions are made, how resources are allocated, and how tasks are handled. This transparency covers everything from administrative processes and volunteer management to how church programs are put into action.

When leaders share this kind of information, it helps everyone understand what's happening behind the scenes and feel more involved in the church's life. This openness not only makes operations more efficient but also strengthens the sense of community and trust among members.

Proverbs 4:7 states, *"Wisdom is the principal thing; therefore get wisdom: and with all thy getting get understanding."* Understanding the operations of the church ensures that members are aware of how their contributions are utilized and how they can be involved in supporting the church's mission.

Leaders can make daily operations more transparent by clearly documenting and sharing how things are done, holding regular check-ins with staff and volunteers, and encouraging open feedback and suggestions. When everyone is kept in the loop and can contribute their thoughts, it helps ensure that the church runs smoothly and efficiently. This kind of openness builds trust and keeps everyone feeling connected and involved in the church's mission.

Effective Communication Strategies

Clear and respectful communication is at the heart of building trust and transparency in the church. It's not just about passing along information; it's also about really listening to the concerns and feedback of the congregation. When we keep the lines of communication open, we prevent misunderstandings and ensure that everyone feels like they're part of the conversation. This approach helps everyone feel informed and involved, creating a more connected and supportive community.

James 1:19 advises us, *"Wherefore, my beloved brethren, let every man be swift to hear, slow to speak, slow to wrath."* This verse highlights the importance of active listening and thoughtful communication, which are crucial for fostering a respectful and transparent environment.

To enhance communication, churches can use several effective strategies. Regular newsletters keep everyone updated on church activities and news, while open forums allow for real-time discussions and feedback. Additionally, feedback surveys offer a way for members to share their thoughts and suggestions. By encouraging open dialogue and providing clear, consistent updates, churches help keep the congregation engaged and well-informed, fostering a stronger and more connected community.

Conclusion

Transparency is a fundamental value that enhances every part of church life. When leaders and members are open about planning, strategy, finances, and operations, it builds a strong foundation of trust and collaboration. This openness not only fosters inclusion and respect but also ensures that the church functions with integrity and effectiveness.

By embracing transparency, we align with biblical principles of honesty and accountability. This creates a church environment where everyone feels informed, involved, and empowered to contribute to our shared mission of serving and growing in faith.

VIII

Maximizing Member Engagement

In a church, every member has a vital role in shaping its direction and success. While leaders make important decisions and offer guidance, the active involvement of everyone—whether they're in formal leadership roles or not—is equally important.

This chapter will explore how empowering all members and recognizing the contributions of lay leaders can make a church community more vibrant and effective. By valuing and encouraging everyone's participation, we build a church where each person feels connected, valued, and motivated to contribute to our shared mission.

Empowering Members

Empowering church members means actively involving them in the church's life and truly valuing their contributions. When members are encouraged to take part in decision-making, it not only makes them feel more connected but also brings in a wide range of perspectives. This inclusivity makes the church stronger and better equipped to meet the needs of its community. By fostering this sense of involvement, we create a more engaged and supportive congregation that works together toward a common purpose.

The Bible supports the idea of shared responsibility and collective input. *1 Corinthians 12:7* says, *"But the manifestation of the Spirit is given to every man to profit withal."* This verse reminds us that every member of the church has a unique gift and role to play. By encouraging active participation, we honor these gifts and foster a more dynamic and engaged church community.

Churches can empower members by involving them in various aspects of church life, from ministry planning to community outreach. Providing opportunities for members to serve on committees, participate in decision-making meetings, and contribute to church projects helps to build a sense of ownership and investment in the church's mission.

Responsibilities of Laity

Lay leaders are the unsung heroes of the church, stepping up to lead and serve even though they don't hold formal ordained positions. They take charge of small groups, organize events, support different ministries, and reach out to the broader community. Their influence is huge because they connect the church's leadership with its members, often acting as a vital link that keeps everyone engaged and informed. Through their dedication and personal touch, lay leaders play a crucial role in energizing the church and fostering a deeper sense of community.

The role of the laity is emphasized in *Ephesians 4:12*, which states, *"For the perfecting of the saints, for the work of the ministry, for the edifying of the body of Christ."* This verse highlights the importance of equipping and empowering all members to contribute to the church's mission. Lay leaders play a critical role in this process, helping to build up the church and ensure its growth and effectiveness.

Understanding the role of lay leaders means acknowledging their valuable contributions and offering the support they need to thrive. It's important to equip them with the right resources and training so they can perform their roles effectively. By encouraging their initiative and providing steady guidance, we help ensure their impact is both positive and meaningful. Supporting lay leaders not only enhances their effectiveness but also enriches the entire church community, making everyone's efforts more impactful and rewarding.

Engaging Members in Governance

Engaging members in governance means involving them in the decisions that guide the church's direction. This goes beyond formal roles like serving on boards or committees—it also includes informal ways to participate, such as joining discussions and providing feedback. When members are actively involved in these processes, they feel a stronger connection to the church's mission and a deeper commitment to its success. This sense of involvement helps foster a more vibrant and unified community, where everyone feels like they're playing a part in shaping the church's future.

Acts 15:22 provides an example of early church governance: *"Then pleased it the apostles and elders, with the whole church, to send chosen men of their own company to Antioch with Paul and Barnabas; namely, Judas surnamed Barsabas, and Silas, chief men among the brethren."* This verse illustrates the practice of involving the entire church in important decisions, highlighting the value of collective input and agreement.

To get members involved in governance, churches can organize regular meetings where key decisions are discussed and feedback is actively sought. Keeping everyone informed about upcoming decisions and providing ample opportunities for input helps ensure that members are not only well-informed but also feel they have a voice in shaping the church's direction. This approach fosters a sense of ownership and engagement, making it easier for members to connect with and contribute to the church's mission.

Building a Culture of Participation

Creating a culture of participation means building an environment where every member feels valued and motivated to get involved. This can be done by celebrating individual contributions, offering various opportunities for engagement, and actively seeking feedback from the congregation. When participation is at the heart of the church's values, it strengthens the sense of community and shared purpose, making everyone feel like they're an essential part of the church's journey.

Hebrews 10:24-25 encourages us to *"consider one another to provoke unto love and to good works: Not forsaking the assembling of ourselves together, as the manner of some is; but exhorting one another: and so much the more, as ye see the day approaching."* This passage underscores the importance of mutual encouragement and participation in the life of the church.

Churches can truly foster a culture of participation by hosting events that bring members together, offering meaningful training and development opportunities, and establishing spaces for open, honest dialogue. When we actively involve everyone and value their input, we not only enhance the church's effectiveness but also build a stronger, more connected community. Let's make it a priority to create an environment where every member feels engaged and valued, and watch our church thrive as a result.

Conclusion

The role of laity and member engagement is crucial for a vibrant and effective church. By empowering members, acknowledging the vital role of lay leaders, and nurturing a culture of participation, churches can build a dynamic and inclusive community. Engaging everyone in the life of the church not only strengthens its mission but also fosters a sense of unity and shared purpose. When we embrace the contributions of every individual, we celebrate the diverse gifts and perspectives that make the church a thriving and living body of Christ.

IX

Gender and Diversity Issues

Creating a church environment that embraces both gender equality and cultural diversity is essential for building a truly inclusive and thriving community. As our society evolves, churches have a golden opportunity to lead the way in demonstrating respect and fairness to everyone. It's not just about implementing policies; it's about fostering a welcoming spirit that reflects Christ's love for all people.

This chapter dives into the heart of gender and diversity issues, offering real, practical approaches to ensure that every member feels valued and engaged. By addressing these complexities with empathy and understanding, we can build a church where every individual's voice is heard, and every person feels they truly belong. Let's explore how we can embrace and celebrate our differences, creating a vibrant and united community that shines as a beacon of love and inclusivity.

Gender Dynamics

Gender dynamics in the church can indeed be intricate, often shaped by cultural and traditional influences. While some churches have made great progress towards gender equality, others are still navigating these challenges. It's crucial to understand and address these dynamics to create an environment where everyone, regardless of gender, has the opportunity to contribute and lead. By tackling these issues head-on, churches can foster a more inclusive and empowering atmosphere, where every individual can fully participate and make a meaningful impact.

1. Historical Context and Scriptural Basis

Historically, many churches have had clear gender roles, often placing men in leadership positions while women took on supportive roles. However, a closer examination of Scripture reveals a more inclusive perspective. For example, *Galatians 3:28* emphasizes the equality of all believers: *"There is neither Jew nor Gentile, neither slave nor free, neither male nor female: for ye are all one in Christ Jesus."* This verse suggests that gender should not be a barrier to serving or leading in the church.

2. Challenges and Opportunities

Despite this scriptural foundation, practical challenges remain. Women and men alike may face obstacles in accessing leadership roles or may encounter bias based on gender. Addressing these challenges involves:

o **Encouraging Women's Leadership**: Many churches are recognizing the value of women in leadership and are actively working to promote women to senior positions. This can include offering leadership training, mentoring programs, and opportunities for women to take on significant roles within the church.

o **Reevaluating Traditional Roles**: Churches may need to reassess traditional gender roles to ensure they align with contemporary understandings of equality. This includes examining roles in preaching, teaching, and administration to ensure all members can participate fully.

o **Addressing Gender Bias**: Actively working to identify and eliminate gender bias in decision-making processes and church policies can help create a more equitable environment. This includes ensuring that hiring practices, leadership opportunities, and congregational roles are open to all, regardless of gender.

3. **Practical Steps for Inclusivity**

To foster gender inclusivity, churches can take several practical steps:

o **Promote Equal Opportunities**: Provide equal opportunities for both men and women in all areas of church life. This includes leadership roles, teaching positions, and administrative functions.

o **Support and Mentor**: Create mentorship programs to support emerging leaders of all genders. Encourage experienced leaders to mentor those who are new to leadership roles.

o **Education and Awareness**: Offer workshops and discussions on gender equality to raise awareness and educate the congregation about the importance of inclusivity.

Cultural and Ethnic Diversity

Cultural and ethnic diversity enriches the church community and reflects the broad spectrum of God's creation. Embracing this diversity is essential for creating a welcoming environment where everyone feels they belong.

1. **Scriptural Foundations for Diversity**

   The Bible emphasizes the importance of inclusivity. *Revelation 7:9* describes a vision of heaven where people from every nation and tongue are gathered together: *"After this I beheld, and, lo, a great multitude, which no man could number, of all nations, and kindreds, and people, and tongues, stood before the throne, and before the Lamb, clothed with white robes, and palms in their hands."* This vision serves as a reminder that God's love and salvation are for all people, regardless of their background.

2. **Addressing Cultural and Ethnic Diversity**

   Churches can take several actions to address and celebrate cultural and ethnic diversity:

   o **Representation in Leadership**: Ensure that church leadership reflects the diversity of the congregation. This can help members from different backgrounds feel represented and valued.
   o **Celebrate Cultural Differences**: Actively celebrate and incorporate different cultural practices into church life. This might include observing various cultural holidays, incorporating diverse music and worship styles, and acknowledging the contributions of different cultural groups.
   o **Foster Inclusivity**: Create an environment where diverse cultural backgrounds are welcomed and respected. This involves being sensitive to different

cultural practices and making efforts to include everyone in church activities.

3. **Promoting Unity Amidst Diversity**

While embracing diversity, it's important to foster unity within the church. This involves:

o **Encouraging Open Dialogue**: Create spaces for open dialogue about cultural and ethnic issues. Encourage members to share their experiences and perspectives in a respectful and constructive manner.
o **Building Relationships**: Promote cross-cultural relationships within the church. Encourage members to engage with one another, learn about different cultures, and build meaningful connections.
o **Addressing Conflict**: Address any conflicts that arise from cultural misunderstandings or biases promptly and with sensitivity. Work to resolve issues in a way that promotes understanding and reconciliation.

Conclusion

Navigating gender and diversity issues in the church requires a genuine commitment to fairness, respect, and inclusivity. By tackling these challenges with thoughtful action and open hearts, churches can foster an environment where every member feels valued and engaged. Embracing gender equality and cultural diversity not only enriches the church community but also mirrors the inclusive nature of God's love. Through intentional efforts and a focus on unity, churches can become beacons of hope and acceptance, truly living out the principles of Scripture in their daily interactions.

X

Financial Stewardship and Transparency

Effective financial stewardship is at the heart of a thriving church. It's not just about balancing the books; it's about ensuring that every dollar supports the church's mission, builds trust with the congregation, and upholds the integrity of the church's operations. Transparent financial practices go beyond mere compliance—they're about honoring the trust and faith that members place in their leaders. In this chapter, we'll dive into the principles of financial accountability and explore practical strategies for managing financial conflicts. We'll also emphasize the importance of transparency, showing how clear and open financial practices can strengthen the entire church community.

Financial Accountability

Financial accountability forms the backbone of responsible church management. It is about making sure that every contribution is used wisely and that the financial practices are open and honest.

1. **Principles of Transparent Financial Management**
   o **Clear Budgeting**: A detailed budget should reflect the church's priorities and mission. This includes planning for various ministries, outreach programs, and operational expenses. Transparency in budgeting involves sharing the budget with the congregation to show how resources are allocated and ensuring that decisions are made with input from various church members.
   o **Regular Reporting**: Providing regular financial reports to the congregation is crucial. These reports should include detailed information about income, expenditures, and any significant changes to the budget. Such transparency helps to prevent misunderstandings and builds trust. As *1 Timothy 5:18* states, *"For the scripture saith, Thou shalt not muzzle the ox that treadeth out the corn. And, The labourer is worthy of his reward."* This verse underscores the importance of fair and clear reporting in acknowledging and valuing the contributions of all.
   o **Accurate Reporting and Periodic Communication**: Accurate reporting involves providing precise and up-to-date financial information. Periodic communication ensures that members are kept informed about the

church's financial status. Leaders should avoid hiding information, as transparency fosters trust and accountability. Although some financial details may be sensitive, a balanced level of transparency is necessary to keep members informed and engaged. This approach aligns with the spirit of *Proverbs 11:1*: *"A false balance is abomination to the Lord: but a just weight is his delight."* Ensuring honesty in financial reporting reflects a commitment to integrity.

Audit and Oversight: Regular audits by an independent party are essential. They provide an objective review of the church's financial practices and can identify areas for improvement. Oversight committees or boards play a critical role in monitoring financial activities and ensuring adherence to best practices.

Ethical Use of Funds: All expenditures should be evaluated to ensure they align with the church's mission and values. Ethical decision-making should guide financial choices, ensuring that every expenditure reflects the church's commitment to its purpose and the responsible use of resources.

Biblical Foundations for Financial Stewardship

The Bible provides clear guidance on financial stewardship. *Proverbs 3:9* encourages us to honor the Lord with our resources: *"Honour the Lord with thy substance, and with the firstfruits of all thine increase."* Additionally, *Luke 16:11* teaches about faithfulness in handling resources: *"If therefore ye have not been faithful in the unrighteous mammon, who will commit to your trust the true riches?"* These principles remind us that managing finances with integrity is a reflection of our faithfulness to God.

Addressing Financial Conflicts

Conflicts over financial matters can arise in any organization, including churches. Effective management of these disputes is essential for maintaining unity and trust within the congregation.

1. **Strategies for Managing Financial Disputes**
   o **Open Communication**: Foster an environment where open and honest discussions about financial matters are encouraged. Leaders should be transparent about financial decisions and willing to address any concerns from the congregation. This openness helps prevent misunderstandings and builds trust within the church community.
   o **Conflict Resolution Mechanisms**: Establish formal mechanisms for addressing financial disputes. This may include setting up a dedicated committee to handle conflicts and ensuring that all parties involved have a chance to present their views. A fair and transparent process is crucial for resolving disputes amicably.
   o **Documentation and Transparency**: Maintain thorough records of all financial transactions and decisions. Transparency in documentation helps clarify the rationale behind financial choices and can resolve disputes more effectively. Sharing these documents

with the congregation, when appropriate, fosters a sense of involvement and trust.

o   **Seek Mediation**: If internal resolution efforts fail, consider engaging an external mediator. An unbiased third party can facilitate discussions and help reach a fair resolution, ensuring that all perspectives are considered.

2. **Maintaining Ethical Financial Practices**

o   **Adherence to Policies**: Develop and follow clear financial policies governing expenditures, reimbursements, and fundraising activities. Regularly review and update these policies to reflect best practices and ensure they remain relevant.

o   **Training and Education**: Provide training for church leaders and staff on financial management and ethical practices. Educating those involved in financial decisions helps prevent errors and ensures that all practices align with established guidelines.

o   **Fostering a Culture of Integrity**: Promote a culture of integrity and accountability within the church. Encourage all members, including leaders and staff, to uphold high standards of honesty and ethical behavior in financial matters.

Conclusion

As we wrap up, it's clear that financial stewardship and transparency are more than just administrative tasks— they are foundational to the health and trustworthiness of the church. By embracing accountability and maintaining open lines of communication, churches can build a strong foundation of trust with their members. Handling financial conflicts with fairness and ethical practices not only upholds the church's integrity but also fosters a culture of respect and stewardship. Ultimately, diligent and transparent financial practices empower the church to fulfill its mission and make a meaningful impact, reflecting its commitment to both God and the community.

XI

The Role of Tradition and Innovation

In the life of any church, the dance between tradition and innovation is both exhilarating and essential. Tradition anchors us, connecting us to the wisdom of our spiritual ancestors and giving us a strong sense of identity. Innovation, however, is the spark that keeps us alive and relevant, helping us meet the shifting needs of our community with fresh ideas and approaches. Navigating this dynamic balance is crucial for a thriving ministry. In this chapter, we'll dive into how churches can honor their rich traditions while embracing the new and exciting possibilities that innovation brings. We'll explore practical ways to blend the old with the new, ensuring that our ministry remains both deeply rooted and vibrantly alive.

Balancing Tradition and Innovation

Traditions within the church serve as the bedrock of our community, grounding us with a sense of continuity and identity. These cherished practices—whether they're ancient hymns, sacred rites, or time-honored ceremonies—are more than just rituals; they're vibrant expressions of our faith and history. They connect us to our past and help us preserve the values that define us.

But as society shifts and grows, so must the church. Embracing innovation isn't about abandoning our roots; it's about breathing new life into them. Innovation helps us adapt our traditions to meet the needs of today's world. For instance, while traditional hymns and liturgies provide comfort and continuity, integrating contemporary music or leveraging digital tools can make worship more relevant and engaging for the present generation.

Navigating this balance between tradition and innovation is essential for a thriving ministry. It's not about choosing one over the other but finding ways to harmonize them. By respecting our rich heritage while also embracing new ideas, we can create a church environment that is both anchored in its values and responsive to the evolving needs of its members. This approach ensures that our practices remain meaningful, and our outreach remains impactful, reflecting a dynamic and living faith.

Balancing these two aspects requires thoughtful reflection. We must ask ourselves how we can honor our traditions while also welcoming new approaches that can invigorate our ministry. The Bible teaches us about seasons and times for change. As *Ecclesiastes 3:1* state, *"To every thing there is a season, and a time to every purpose under the heaven."* This verse reminds us that change is a natural part of life, including in our spiritual practices.

Navigating the Tension

Finding harmony between tradition and innovation often involves careful and respectful dialogue. It's important to approach this balance with a heart open to both preserving what is meaningful and exploring what is new. Here are a few principles to guide this process:

- **Honor the Past**: Traditions are valuable because they connect us to our spiritual heritage. They help ground our faith and offer a sense of belonging. As *2 Thessalonians 2:15* encourages, *"Therefore, brethren, stand fast, and hold the traditions which ye have been taught, whether by word, or our epistle."* Respecting these practices helps maintain a link to our past.
- **Embrace New Ideas**: At the same time, we need to be open to innovation. The world changes, and so do the needs of our congregations. New methods or technologies can enhance our mission without negating the value of tradition. For example, using social media to share sermons or connect with the community can

complement, rather than replace, traditional forms of outreach.

3. **Engage the Congregation**: It's crucial to involve the congregation in discussions about changes. By listening to their thoughts and concerns, leaders can implement innovations in ways that are thoughtful and considerate. *Proverbs 15:22* reminds us, *"Without counsel purposes are disappointed: but in the multitude of counsellors, they are established."* This highlights the importance of seeking collective input.

4. **Integrate Gradually**: Introducing new practices gradually allows the congregation to adjust and embrace changes without feeling overwhelmed. It's about finding a rhythm that respects the past while moving forward.

5. **Combine the Old and the New**: Look for ways to merge traditional and contemporary practices. For instance, combining classic hymns with modern worship styles can create a service that honors tradition while also appealing to current tastes.

Innovations in Church Governance

Innovation in church governance involves exploring new models and approaches to leadership. Here are some ways churches are creatively adapting their governance structures:

1. **Collaborative Leadership**: Some churches are shifting towards more collaborative leadership models, where decision-making is shared among various leaders. This

can lead to more diverse perspectives and a more inclusive decision-making process. As the early church demonstrated in *Acts 6:3, "Wherefore, brethren, look ye out among you seven men of honest report, full of the Holy Ghost and wisdom, whom we may appoint over this business."* Shared leadership allows for a broader range of insights and experiences.

2. **Digital Tools**: The integration of technology has transformed how churches operate. From virtual meetings to online donation systems, technology can improve efficiency and outreach. It allows for greater connectivity and can make church activities more accessible to those unable to attend in person.

3. **Community Outreach**: Innovation in outreach efforts can involve forming new partnerships with local organizations or adopting novel approaches to community service. This might include developing programs that address contemporary social issues or exploring creative ways to engage with the local community.

4. **Adaptive Worship**: Updating worship practices to include multimedia presentations or interactive elements can enhance the experience for modern congregants while preserving essential elements of traditional worship.

Conclusion

The dance between tradition and innovation is at the heart of a church's journey, driving its growth and vitality. Cherished traditions ground us in our spiritual heritage, offering a sense of identity and continuity. Meanwhile, thoughtful innovation breathes new life into these practices, allowing us to engage with and address the ever-changing needs of our community.

By blending respect for our past with a willingness to adapt, we create a vibrant faith community that honors its roots while staying relevant. This dynamic balance not only preserves the essence of our beliefs but also ensures that we are equipped to meet the present with enthusiasm and insight. Embracing both tradition and innovation with a spirit of grace and wisdom helps our church remain a beacon of hope and relevance, guiding us effectively through the complexities of today's world.

XII

Church Governance

Effective church governance is the backbone of a well-functioning and impactful ministry. It sets the stage for making sound decisions, managing responsibilities, and overseeing resources. In this chapter, we'll dive into the core elements of governance that keep a church running smoothly, from thorough documentation and clear standard operating procedures (SOPs) to regular review meetings and key performance indicators (KPIs).

We'll also explore the importance of establishing terms of reference, resolving conflicts, maintaining transparency, and conducting audits. These practices are not just administrative necessities—they are grounded in biblical principles that guide church leadership and administration. By embracing these elements, churches can build a robust governance framework that supports both their spiritual mission and practical needs.

Importance of Proper Documentation

Documentation is the backbone of good governance. It ensures that decisions, policies, and procedures are recorded and can be referenced when needed. Proper documentation includes meeting minutes, financial reports, policy manuals, and operational guidelines. For instance, keeping detailed minutes of meetings helps ensure that decisions made are clearly recorded and can be reviewed later. *Proverbs 16:3* teaches us to commit our plans to the Lord: *"Commit thy works unto the Lord, and thy thoughts shall be established."* This principle reminds us that meticulous documentation aligns our actions with our commitments.

Standard Operating Procedures (SOPs)

Standard Operating Procedures (SOPs) are detailed instructions that outline how specific tasks should be carried out. They help ensure consistency and efficiency in church operations. For example, an SOP for handling financial transactions might specify how to process donations, manage receipts, and handle deposits. This is especially important when staff members leave or new ones are hired, as SOPs ensure that essential tasks are performed consistently and accurately. *1 Corinthians 14:40* emphasizes order: *"Let all things be done decently and in order."* Having clear SOPs helps maintain this order and ensures that operations continue smoothly.

Review Meetings

Regular review meetings are crucial for assessing progress and addressing issues. These meetings provide a platform for leaders to discuss accomplishments, identify challenges, and set future goals. For example, a quarterly review meeting might include evaluating the success of recent events, discussing budget performance, and planning upcoming activities. *Proverbs 27:23* advises: *"Be thou diligent to know the state of thy flocks and look well to thy herds."* Regular reviews help church leaders stay informed and make necessary adjustments to meet their goals.

Key Performance Indicators (KPIs) and Targets

Key Performance Indicators (KPIs) are measurable values that help track the effectiveness of church activities. KPIs might include metrics such as attendance numbers, financial contributions, or the number of community outreach programs. Setting clear targets for these KPIs helps focus efforts and drive progress. For instance, a KPI might be to increase community engagement by 20% over the next year.

Philippians 3:14 encourages us to press toward our goals: *"I press toward the mark for the prize of the high calling of God in Christ Jesus."* KPIs and targets help churches pursue their mission with determination and purpose.

Terms of Reference

Terms of Reference (ToR) define the scope, responsibilities, and authority of committees, boards, and roles within the church. They clarify what each group or individual is expected to do and the limits of their authority. For example, a ToR for a finance committee might outline their responsibilities for budgeting, financial reporting, and oversight of expenditures. *Ecclesiastes 3:1* states: *"To everything there is a season, and a time to every purpose under the heaven."* Clear Terms of Reference ensure that every role and responsibility is managed effectively and in accordance with its purpose.

Conflict Resolution Procedures

Having established procedures for conflict resolution is essential for maintaining harmony within the church. These procedures should be fair, transparent, and biblically grounded. For example, a church might adopt a process outlined in *Matthew 18:15*: *"Moreover if thy brother shall trespass against thee, go and tell him his fault between thee and him alone."* This approach helps resolve disputes in a respectful and constructive manner, fostering unity and trust among members.

Transparency in Decision-Making

Transparency is key to building trust and fostering a healthy church environment. Leaders should openly communicate how decisions are made and the reasons behind them. This includes sharing information about planning, strategy, finances, and operations. For example, making financial reports accessible to members and discussing major decisions in open forums can help prevent misunderstandings and build trust. *2 Corinthians 8:21* emphasizes the importance of honesty: *"Providing for honest things, not only in the sight of the Lord, but also in the sight of men."* Transparency helps ensure that members feel valued and involved.

Regular Audits and Evaluations

Regular audits and evaluations help assess the effectiveness of church operations and ensure that resources are used wisely. Audits might include reviewing financial records, evaluating program outcomes, and assessing compliance with policies. *1 Corinthians 4:2* underscores the need for accountability: *"Moreover it is required in stewards, that a man be found faithful."* Regular audits and evaluations promote a culture of stewardship and help identify areas for improvement.

Effective Communication Channels

Establishing clear communication channels is essential for keeping everyone informed and engaged. This includes having regular updates, open forums for discussion, and accessible communication tools. For instance, using newsletters, social media, and regular meetings can help ensure that members are aware of church activities and decisions. *Ephesians 4:29* encourages constructive communication: *"Let no corrupt communication proceed out of your mouth, but that which is good to the use of edifying, that it may minister grace unto the hearers."* Effective communication helps build a connected and informed church community.

Ethical Fundraising and Financial Management

Ethical fundraising and financial management are crucial for maintaining trust and integrity. Churches should follow best practices for raising and using funds, ensuring that all activities are conducted transparently and ethically. For example, clearly outlining how funds will be used and providing regular updates on financial status helps maintain transparency. *2 Corinthians 9:7* highlights the importance of integrity in giving: *"Every man according as he purposeth in his heart, so let him give; not grudgingly, or of necessity: for God loveth a cheerful giver."* Ethical financial practices ensure that members' contributions are respected and used effectively.

Conclusion

Effective church governance goes beyond just having rules and procedures—it's about fostering a culture of transparency, accountability, and integrity. By putting in place solid documentation, clear SOPs, regular review meetings, and meaningful KPIs, churches lay the groundwork for smooth and effective operations. Adding in well-defined Terms of Reference, proactive conflict resolution, and ethical financial practices brings everything together. These elements aren't just administrative; they're about living out our mission and values in a way that truly resonates with the congregation. Embracing these principles helps churches build trust, operate with excellence, and reflect the wisdom and love that guide our faith.

XIII

Congregational Care and Support

As we dive into the heart of what makes a church truly thrive, let's focus on two vital areas: Congregational Care and Community Outreach. These are more than just tasks—they're the lifeblood of a vibrant, impactful church.

In this chapter, we'll explore how to nurture our members with heartfelt pastoral care and counseling, ensuring that everyone feels supported and valued.

We'll also look at how to extend our reach into the wider community, demonstrating our commitment to making a real difference in the world. By investing in both our own congregation and our broader community, we can build a church that not only supports its members but also actively contributes to the well-being of those around us.

PASTORAL CARE AND COUNSELING

Introduction to Pastoral Care

Pastoral care is all about providing emotional and spiritual support to church members. It's about being there for people in their times of need, offering guidance, and creating a nurturing environment. Effective pastoral care helps individuals navigate life's challenges, strengthens their faith, and builds a supportive church community.

Counseling Strategies

- **Listening Skills:** Active listening is a key part of pastoral care. It means really focusing on what someone is saying, understanding their feelings, and responding with empathy. This helps build trust and ensures that people feel valued and heard.

2. **Emotional Support:** Offering emotional support means being there for people with empathy and understanding. It's about providing comfort and encouragement during tough times and helping individuals feel less alone in their struggles.
3. **Spiritual Guidance:** Guiding people in their faith journey is another crucial aspect. This involves helping them connect with their beliefs, offering prayer, and providing biblical insights that bring hope and clarity.
4. **Crisis Intervention:** In emergencies, pastors need to offer immediate support. This might include being a listening ear, providing practical help, or connecting individuals with additional resources like professional counseling.

Case Study: Unseen Support

Here's a story that illustrates the power of pastoral care. There was a pastor I knew who exemplified selfless leadership. Despite facing personal and financial difficulties, he never shared these struggles with his congregation or asked for help. His dedication to his ministry was evident, as he continued to serve others faithfully, even while dealing with his own challenges.

A group of observant congregants noticed the pastor's quiet struggle and felt compelled to act. Without making his situation public, they discreetly organized support for him. They arranged anonymous donations, prepared a care package with essentials, and coordinated help with his physical needs.

This support had a profound effect on the pastor. It not only relieved his immediate concerns but also showed him how much his congregation appreciated and cared for him. This act of kindness strengthened the bond between the pastor and the congregation, fostering a greater sense of unity and mutual support within the church.

This story highlights the importance of recognizing and addressing the needs of leaders, even when they don't explicitly ask for help. It shows how compassion and discreet support can make a real difference and deepen the sense of community within the church. This is the same feeling that a member of the church feels when such care is also brought upon those in need within the church, not for pastors only.

COMMUNITY OUTREACH AND SOCIAL RESPONSIBILITY

The Role of the Church in Community Engagement

Churches play a significant role in their communities. Engaging in outreach and social responsibility helps address local needs, promotes justice, and shows the church's commitment to serving others.

Outreach Strategies

- **Local Initiatives:** Organize events and programs that tackle local issues. This might include food drives, health fairs, or educational workshops. Tailoring initiatives to the community's specific needs ensures they are impactful and relevant.

2. **Partnerships:** Collaborate with other organizations and charities. Working together can amplify the church's efforts and provide additional resources and support.

3. **Volunteer Opportunities:** Encourage congregants to get involved in community service. Offering various ways to participate, such as mission trips or local volunteering, fosters a culture of service and generosity.

Social Responsibility

1. **Advocacy and Justice:** Address social issues like poverty and inequality from a faith perspective. Advocate for positive change and support initiatives that promote justice and equity.

2. **Sustainable Practices:** Implement eco-friendly practices in church operations and encourage congregants to adopt sustainable habits. This shows a commitment to caring for God's creation and responsibility towards future generations.

Success Stories

At one time, our church faced challenges with divisions and low engagement among members. However, when the pastor and some of the leaders took the initiative to practice outreach sessions specifically for the existing members, there was a remarkable turnaround. These outreach efforts led to increased activity engagement and stronger commitments from the congregation.

By focusing on re-engaging existing members through targeted outreach, the church was able to revive its sense of community and involvement. This example highlights the effectiveness of proactive outreach in revitalizing church life and fostering greater commitment among members.

INTEGRATING CONGREGATIONAL CARE AND COMMUNITY SUPPORT

Holistic Approach

Balancing individual care with community outreach creates a comprehensive support system. Both aspects are interconnected and contribute to a healthier and more vibrant church community.

Building a Supportive Network

Foster a church culture that values both internal support and external engagement. Encouraging open communication and mutual support helps build a strong, unified congregation.

Evaluating Effectiveness

Regularly assess the impact of pastoral care and outreach efforts. Collect feedback, measure outcomes, adjust and enhance effectiveness and address emerging needs.

Conclusion

Effective congregational care and community outreach are the heartbeats of a thriving church. When we pour our energy into compassionate pastoral care and actively engage with our community, we create an environment where everyone feels supported and valued. Balancing these elements not only strengthens our internal bonds but also extends our impact beyond the church walls.

By committing ourselves to genuinely care for each other and make a positive difference in the broader community, we embody the spirit of our shared values and aspirations. Let's move forward with dedication, reflecting the best of our mission and truly making a difference in the lives of those we serve.

XIV

Leadership Development and Mentorship

As churches grow and evolve, nurturing the next generation of leaders becomes essential to maintaining a vibrant and dynamic community. This chapter will explore how we can identify emerging leaders and cultivate their potential through meaningful mentorship. We'll delve into strategies for building robust mentorship programs that not only guide and inspire but also empower individuals to take on leadership roles with confidence and vision. By investing in the growth of future leaders, we ensure that our church remains resilient and forward-thinking, ready to meet the challenges and opportunities of tomorrow.

IDENTIFYING AND NURTURING FUTURE LEADERS

Spotting Potential Leaders

1. **Watching for Commitment:** Potential leaders often shine through their dedication. Look for those who are always involved, volunteering for various tasks, and showing genuine enthusiasm for church activities. Their consistent presence and initiative are clear signs of their potential.

   "Well done, good and faithful servant; you have been faithful over a little; I will set you over much." — Matthew 25:23

2. **Evaluating Skills and Talents:** Keep an eye on those who have the skills needed for leadership—strong communication, the ability to inspire others, and a

knack for problem-solving. Identifying these traits early can help guide them towards leadership roles.

"The gift you have received; use it to serve others, as faithful stewards of God's grace in its various forms." — 1 Peter 4:10

3. **Assessing Character:** True leadership requires solid character. Look for people who are reliable, humble, and compassionate. How they handle challenges and interact with others can reveal a lot about their readiness to lead.

"The righteous who walks in his integrity—blessed are his children after him!" — Proverbs 20:7

Developing Future Leaders

. **Providing Opportunities:** Give potential leaders chances to step up. Let them lead small groups, organize events, or get involved in decision-making. These experiences build their confidence and help them develop their leadership skills.

"So I exhort the elders among you, as a fellow elder and a witness of the sufferings of Christ, as well as a partaker in the glory that is going to be revealed: shepherd the flock of God that is among you, exercising oversight." — 1 Peter 5:1-2

. **Offering Training:** Invest in their growth by providing training on leadership skills. Workshops on public speaking, conflict resolution, and planning can make a big difference. These resources prepare individuals for future leadership roles.

"The heart of the discerning acquires knowledge; the ears of the wise seek it out." — Proverbs 18:15

3. **Encouraging Growth:** Foster an environment that supports ongoing personal and spiritual growth. Encourage them to pursue further education, read relevant books, and seek mentorship. Continuous growth is essential for effective leadership.

"Iron sharpens iron, and one man sharpens another." — Proverbs 27:17

MENTORSHIP PROGRAMS

Creating Effective Mentorship Programs

1. **Designing the Program:** Define what you want to achieve with your mentorship program. Set clear goals, whether it's developing specific skills or preparing individuals for leadership roles. Clear objectives help both mentors and mentees understand their roles.

"Commit your work to the Lord, and your plans will be established." — Proverbs 16:3

2. **Selecting Mentors:** Choose mentors who are experienced and willing to guide others. They should be

approachable, knowledgeable, and committed to helping others grow.

"Let the elders who rule well be considered worthy of double honor, especially those who labor in preaching and teaching." — 1 Timothy 5:17

Pairing Mentors and Mentees: Match mentors and mentees based on their interests, skills, and needs. Compatibility in working style and personality ensures productive and supportive relationships.

"Two are better than one, because they have a good reward for their toil." — Ecclesiastes 4:9

Implementing the Program

Setting Up Regular Meetings: Schedule consistent meetings between mentors and mentees. Regular interaction helps with goal setting, feedback, and tracking progress.

"As iron sharpens iron, so one person sharpens another." — Proverbs 27:17

Providing Resources: Equip both mentors and mentees with resources like guidelines and training materials. This structure helps make the mentorship process effective and focused.

"And he gave the apostles, the prophets, the evangelists, the shepherds and teachers, to equip the

saints for the work of ministry, for building up the body of Christ." — Ephesians 4:11-12

3. **Evaluating Progress:** Regularly review the mentorship program. Gather feedback, assess progress, and adjust program to be beneficial for everyone involved.

"Let all things be done decently and in order." — 1 Corinthians 14:40

Success Stories

Let me share my own story as an example of how mentorship can transform lives. I am a product of leadership development and mentorship. Before becoming a pastor, I worked under various pastors and leaders. Through observing their actions and being guided in my tasks, I learned the ropes of church leadership and counseling. I watched how things were done and then had the chance to practice these skills myself. This hands-on experience was crucial in shaping my leadership abilities and preparing me for my role today.

INTEGRATING LEADERSHIP DEVELOPMENT AND MENTORSHIP

Creating a Culture of Leadership

Encourage a culture that values leadership growth. Help everyone see themselves as potential leaders and provide clear paths for their development.

"The greatest among you shall be your servant." — Matthew 23:11

Ongoing Support and Feedback

Make sure mentors and mentees receive ongoing support and feedback. Regular communication helps address any issues and keeps the mentorship relationship strong.

"Let the word of Christ dwell in you richly, teaching and admonishing one another in all wisdom." — Colossians 3:16

Celebrating Achievements

Celebrate the successes of emerging leaders and the accomplishments of the mentorship program. Recognizing progress motivates everyone and highlights the importance of investing in leadership development.

"Rejoice in the Lord always; again, I will say, rejoice." — Philippians 4:4

Conclusion

Cultivating effective leadership and mentorship is not just a strategy—it's a commitment to the future of our church. By identifying and nurturing emerging leaders and establishing robust mentorship programs, we lay the foundation for a strong and vibrant leadership team. This investment in our future leaders equips them with the tools and confidence they need to guide our church with passion and vision. As we support and celebrate their growth, we ensure that our church community remains dynamic and thriving. Together, let's build a legacy of leadership that reflects our shared values and strengthens our mission for years to come.

XV

Crisis Management and Resilience

Every church encounters crises—times that test our strength and unity. How we prepare for and navigate these challenges can profoundly impact the resilience of our community. In this chapter, we'll explore how to develop robust crisis management plans and foster a resilient congregation. Our goal is to turn these trying moments into opportunities for growth and renewal, strengthening our church's ability to support one another and emerge stronger than before. Let's delve into strategies that not only address the immediate needs during a crisis but also build a foundation for lasting resilience and unity.

Developing Crisis Management Plans

1. **Assess Potential Risks:** Identify the types of crises your church might encounter, whether it's a natural disaster, financial trouble, or leadership issues. By understanding these risks, you can create plans tailored to each scenario.

   "The wise man sees danger and hides himself, but the simple go on and suffer for it." — Proverbs 22:3

2. **Create a Crisis Response Team:** Put together a diverse team from within the church. Include leaders, counselors, and administrators, each bringing unique skills to the table. Clear roles and responsibilities ensure swift action when a crisis hits.

   "Plans are established by counsel; by wise guidance wage war." — Proverbs 20:18

3. **Develop Action Plans:** Draft detailed procedures for various crisis scenarios. This includes evacuation routes, communication strategies, and support steps for those affected. Make sure these plans are easy to access and keep them updated.

   "The prudent sees danger and hides himself, but the simple go on and suffer for it." — Proverbs 27:12

4. **Communicate Effectively:** Set up clear channels for crisis communication. Use text alerts, emails, and social media to keep everyone informed and involved. Transparency builds trust and keeps the congregation united.

"Let your speech always be gracious, seasoned with salt, so that you may know how you ought to answer each person." — Colossians 4:6

Training and Drills

1. **Conduct Regular Training:** Ensure the crisis response team is well-prepared through ongoing training. Host workshops and drills to practice responses, improving coordination and efficiency.

"And let the peace of Christ rule in your hearts, to which indeed you were called in one body. And be thankful." — Colossians 3:15

2. **Run Simulation Exercises:** Organize realistic drills to test your crisis management plans. These exercises reveal weaknesses and offer a chance to refine your strategies.

"The plans of the diligent lead surely to abundance, but everyone who is hasty comes only to poverty." — Proverbs 21:5

Review and Revise: After each drill or real crisis, review what worked and what didn't. Update your plans based on these insights to keep your response strategies sharp.

"A wise man will hear and increase in learning, and a man of understanding will acquire wise counsel." — Proverbs 1:5

BUILDING RESILIENCE IN THE CONGREGATION

Fostering a Supportive Community

1. **Promote Open Communication:** Encourage honest conversations within the church. Provide spaces where members can share their concerns, seek help, and support one another. Open dialogue strengthens relationships and fosters trust.

   "Bear one another's burdens, and so fulfill the law of Christ." — Galatians 6:2

2. **Provide Emotional and Spiritual Support:** Offer counseling, prayer support, and practical help. Equip your congregation with the resources they need to navigate their challenges.

   "Cast all your anxiety on him because he cares for you." — 1 Peter 5:7

3. **Encourage Community Involvement:** Get members involved in volunteer work and community service. Active participation boosts morale and fosters a sense of belonging.

"And let us not grow weary of doing good, for in due season we will reap, if we do not give up." — Galatians 6:9

Strengthening Spiritual Foundations

1. **Focus on Faith and Hope:** Use sermons, Bible studies, and devotional materials to reinforce faith and hope. Encourage your congregation to rely on their spiritual strength during tough times.

"The Lord is my refuge and strength, an ever-present help in trouble." — Psalm 46:1

2. **Build a Culture of Resilience:** Make resilience a core value of your church. Teach members to lean on their faith and support each other, showing that they are stronger together.

"But the one who endures to the end will be saved." — Matthew 24:13

3. **Celebrate Recovery and Growth:** Recognize and celebrate the progress made after a crisis. Share stories of recovery and growth to inspire and uplift your community.

"Rejoice in hope, be patient in tribulation, be constant in prayer." — Romans 12:12

Success Stories

Financial crises are all too common in churches, especially in Africa. Our church once faced a severe financial shortfall that threatened our operations. In response, an emergency team of leaders sprang into action, devising strategies to raise additional funds and manage expenses. Their quick thinking and collaborative efforts turned a daunting situation into a success story. Through this experience, our congregation not only overcame the financial challenge but emerged stronger and more united, demonstrating the power of effective crisis management and resilience.

Conclusion

Navigating crises and building resilience are not just tasks but opportunities to strengthen the heart of our church community. When we prepare with foresight, communicate with honesty, and rally around each other, we transform challenges into catalysts for growth. Let's embrace the process of crafting thoughtful crisis management plans and nurturing a supportive environment. By reinforcing our spiritual roots and standing united, we can turn adversity into a testament of our faith and collective strength. Together, we'll face every storm with courage, turning each challenge into a chance to grow and shine brighter than ever.

XVI

Ecumenical and Interfaith Relations

In an increasingly interconnected world, the call to reach out and build relationships beyond our own church walls has never been more important. This chapter explores deep into the rich opportunities that arise from engaging with other faith communities and collaborating across denominations. By extending our hands and hearts beyond our own congregations, we open doors to deeper understanding, greater unity, and a stronger collective impact. Together, we'll explore how these connections can enrich our faith journey, broaden our perspectives, and amplify the positive influence we can have in the world. Let's embrace the power of collaboration and celebrate the shared mission that binds us all.

BUILDING RELATIONSHIPS WITH OTHER FAITH COMMUNITIES

Starting Conversations

1. **Reach Out with Curiosity:** Begin by reaching out to leaders from different faith traditions. Approach these conversations with genuine curiosity and respect, eager to learn about their beliefs and practices.

   "How good and pleasant it is when God's people live together in unity!" — Psalm 133:1

2. **Find Common Ground:** Focus on shared values such as community service, peace, and justice. Highlighting these common goals helps build a strong foundation for meaningful dialogue.

   "Let us not give up meeting together, but encourage one another." — Hebrews 10:25

3. **Host Joint Events:** Organize events that bring together people from different faith backgrounds. These could include community service projects, discussion forums, or educational sessions. They're great ways to promote understanding and work together on shared goals.

   "The heart of man plans his way, but the Lord establishes his steps." — Proverbs 16:9

Fostering Mutual Respect

Respect Differences: Embrace and honor the differences between faith traditions. Approach these differences with sensitivity and a willingness to learn, rather than to judge.

"Be kind and compassionate to one another, forgiving each other, just as in Christ God forgave you." — Ephesians 4:32

Learn and Grow Together: Use these interactions as opportunities to learn from each other. Mutual learning helps break down stereotypes and build deeper connections.

"My people are destroyed for lack of knowledge." — Hosea 4:6

Promote Inclusivity: Ensure that everyone feels valued and heard. Create spaces where people from all backgrounds can come together and share their perspectives.

"For there is no distinction between Jew and Greek; the same Lord is Lord of all." — Romans 10:12

PROMOTING UNITY ACROSS DENOMINATIONS

Working Together with Other Christian Denominations

1. **Focus on Shared Missions:** Identify and work towards common goals, such as community outreach and support for those in need. Shared missions can unite different denominations and drive collaborative efforts.

   "For where two or three gather in my name, there am I with them." — Matthew 18:20

2. **Encourage Open Dialogue:** Foster honest and open dialogue between different Christian groups. This can help address theological differences and find common ground on which to work together.

   "Make every effort to keep the unity of the Spirit through the bond of peace." — Ephesians 4:3

3. **Plan Ecumenical Events:** Host events that bring together various Christian denominations for worship, prayer, and fellowship. These gatherings help build relationships and strengthen unity.

   "Let us therefore make every effort to do what leads to peace and to mutual edification." — Romans 14:19

4. **Support Interdenominational Projects:** Collaborate on ministries and programs that cross denominational

lines. This could include joint worship services, educational programs, or community service projects.

"And let us not grow weary of doing good, for in due season we will reap if we do not give up." — Galatians 6:9

Building Strong Partnerships

1. **Develop Long-Term Relationships:** Focus on building lasting relationships with other denominations. Regular interaction helps maintain unity and deepens connections.

   "As iron sharpens iron, so one person sharpens another." — Proverbs 27:17

2. **Celebrate Successes Together:** Acknowledge and celebrate the achievements of joint efforts. Celebrating successes fosters a sense of camaraderie and encourages continued collaboration.

   "Rejoice with those who rejoice; mourn with those who mourn." — Romans 12:15

3. **Handle Conflicts with Grace:** Address disagreements with a spirit of reconciliation and understanding. Focus on resolving issues in a way that respects different viewpoints while keeping common goals in mind.

   "If it is possible, as far as it depends on you, live at peace with everyone." — Romans 12:18

Success Stories

In my journey as a youth pastor, I've discovered the profound impact of connecting with other faith communities. Collaborating on shared projects and engaging in interfaith dialogues has not only deepened our understanding but also forged lasting bonds. These partnerships have illuminated the fact that, despite our varied traditions and names, we are all united in Christ's love. Working together toward common goals has not only strengthened our relationships but also showcased the incredible power of unity to drive meaningful change and foster a spirit of shared purpose.

Conclusion

Engaging with other faith communities and bridging denominational divides is crucial for nurturing deeper understanding and unity in today's diverse world. When we reach out with genuine respect, align our efforts with shared missions, and celebrate our joint achievements, we build not just stronger connections but also more compassionate communities. Let's embrace these opportunities to collaborate and appreciate the beautiful tapestry of faith that unites us all, creating a vibrant, supportive network that reflects the true spirit of togetherness and shared purpose.

XVII

Legal and Ethical Considerations

When it comes to church leadership, handling legal and ethical responsibilities is more than just a formality—it's essential for maintaining trust and smooth operations. Many churches overlook the need for a dedicated legal arm within their board or administration. However, having legal expertise readily available can make all the difference, especially when navigating complex issues. In this chapter, we'll explore why understanding legal obligations and making ethical decisions is crucial and share some real-life examples of how these practices can save the day.

UNDERSTANDING LEGAL OBLIGATIONS

Employment Laws

1. **Complying with Employment Regulations:** Just like any other organization, churches need to follow employment laws. This means fair hiring practices, creating a non-discriminatory environment, and ensuring a safe workplace for all staff. Knowing and adhering to these regulations helps keep the church a fair and respectful place to work.

   "You shall not pervert the justice due to your poor in his lawsuit." — Exodus 23:6

2. **Keeping Accurate Records:** Maintaining detailed records of employment contracts, salaries, and working hours is crucial. It's not only about compliance; it's also about transparency and fairness.

   "The integrity of the upright guides them, but the crookedness of the treacherous destroys them." — Proverbs 11:3

3. **Addressing Employment Issues:** Have clear procedures in place for handling complaints and disputes. A well-defined process for resolving conflicts ensures fairness and builds trust within the church.

   "Let justice roll down like waters and righteousness like an ever-flowing stream." — Amos 5:24

Property Regulations

. **Understanding Property Laws:** Churches must be aware of local regulations concerning property use, zoning, and building codes. This helps avoid legal trouble and ensures that church property is used correctly.

"Give justice to the weak and the fatherless; maintain the right of the afflicted and the destitute." — Psalm 82:3

. **Managing Property Transactions:** Whether buying, selling, or leasing property, follow legal procedures to ensure everything is done properly. Doing your homework and getting the necessary approvals can prevent costly mistakes.

"The plans of the diligent lead surely to abundance, but everyone who is hasty comes only to poverty." — Proverbs 21:5

. **Safeguarding Church Assets:** Protect your church's assets with appropriate insurance and risk management. This not only prevents financial loss but also ensures the church can continue its mission without interruption.

"The prudent see danger and take refuge, but the simple keep going and pay the penalty." — Proverbs 22:3

ETHICAL DECISION-MAKING

Navigating Complex Ethical Dilemmas

1. **Establish Clear Ethical Guidelines:** A well-defined code of ethics helps guide decision-making in line with the church's values. This clarity is essential for making decisions that reflect your church's mission.

   "The righteous will never be removed, but the wicked will not dwell in the land." — Proverbs 10:30

2. **Consult Trusted Advisors:** When faced with difficult choices, seek advice from mentors or advisors. Their experience and wisdom can offer valuable guidance and help you make decisions that align with your church's values.

   "Plans are established by counsel; by wise guidance wage war." — Proverbs 20:18

3. **Consider the Impact:** Think through how your decisions will affect everyone involved—members, staff, and the community. Aim to make choices that are fair and beneficial for all.

   "Let each of you look not only to his own interests, but also to the interests of others." — Philippians 2:4

4. **Promote Transparency:** Being open about how decisions are made helps build trust and shows that you are committed to acting with integrity.

"But let your 'Yes' be 'Yes,' and your 'No,' 'No,' so that you may not fall under condemnation." — James 5:12

Handling Ethical Conflicts

1. **Address Conflicts Quickly:** When ethical issues arise, tackle them head-on. Addressing problems promptly prevents them from growing and demonstrates a commitment to doing what's right.

"If a brother or sister is poorly clothed and lacking in daily food, and one of you says to them, 'Go in peace, be warmed and filled,' without giving them the things needed for the body, what good is that?" — James 2:15-16

. **Uphold Core Values:** Stick to your church's core values even when decisions are tough. This consistency helps maintain integrity and builds trust within the community.

"The integrity of the upright guides them, but the crookedness of the treacherous destroys them." — Proverbs 11:3

. **Encourage an Ethical Culture:** Foster a culture where ethical behavior is expected and rewarded. Provide training and encourage discussions about ethics to help everyone make sound decisions.

"The wicked flee when no one pursues, but the righteous are bold as a lion." — Proverbs 28:1

Success Stories

Let me share a powerful moment from our journey. Our church once encountered a significant legal challenge when a former employee pursued legal action over post-employment issues. It was an intimidating situation, and none of us had a clue how to navigate it. But, in that moment of uncertainty, we turned to the legal experts within our congregation. Their guidance was nothing short of a lifeline—it saved us both substantial resources and safeguarded our church's reputation. This experience highlighted just how critical it is for churches to have legal knowledge and resources on standby. It's a reminder of the immense value of embracing legal and ethical standards and having skilled professionals ready to guide us through the complexities that arise. This also shows how valuable every member in a congregation matters, everyone has a part to play.

Conclusion

Handling legal and ethical responsibilities is essential for preserving the integrity of church operations. By thoroughly understanding and adhering to employment and property laws, and by making thoughtful ethical decisions, churches can uphold their mission and foster a positive, respectful environment. Let's embrace these principles wholeheartedly, ensuring our churches remain beacons of fairness and integrity, shining brightly within our communities.

XVIII

Technology and Church Leadership

In today's fast-paced world, technology is no longer just a convenience—it's transforming how we connect, communicate, and worship. Many churches, however, tend to shy away from it, thinking it's not crucial for ministry. But the truth is, times have changed, and technology is a tool that can no longer be ignored. It's essential to embrace it and utilize it to its full potential to keep our ministries vibrant and relevant in this digital age.

HARNESSING DIGITAL COMMUNICATION

Social Media Engagement

Social media platforms like Facebook, Instagram, and Twitter aren't just for sharing pictures or catching up with friends—they're powerful tools for spreading the Gospel and keeping your congregation engaged.

Building an online presence allows you to reach not just the people sitting in the pews but also those who may not attend church regularly. By sharing inspirational messages, event updates, and even a glimpse into the behind-the-scenes life of your church, you can create a lively online community that extends far beyond Sunday mornings.

"Go into all the world and preach the gospel to all creation." — Mark 16:15

And it's not just about posting content—engage with your audience! Host live Q&A sessions, create polls, and start discussion threads. These interactive elements invite your congregation to participate actively, fostering a sense of belonging and community even online.

"Let your light shine before others, that they may see your good deeds and glorify your Father in heaven." — *Matthew 5:16*

Email Newsletters and Digital Bulletins

Emails aren't dead—they're a direct line of communication that your congregation can access anytime, anywhere. Regular email newsletters and digital bulletins keep everyone informed about upcoming events, sermon series, and community activities.

"Let your conversation be always full of grace, seasoned with salt, so that you may know how to answer everyone." — Colossians 4:6

Take it a step further by personalizing these messages. Send targeted emails based on members' interests and involvement. This approach not only makes communication more relevant but also shows that you care about each individual's spiritual journey.

"Therefore encourage one another and build each other up, just as in fact you are doing." — 1 Thessalonians 5:11

ONLINE WORSHIP AND STREAMING SERVICES

Live Streaming Sermons

For those who can't make it to church—whether due to health reasons, distance, or other commitments—live streaming offers a way to stay connected. With platforms like YouTube, Facebook Live, and Zoom, broadcasting your services has never been easier.

"For where two or three gather in my name, there am I with them." — Matthew 18:20

And the beauty of online services is their flexibility. Record your sermons and make them available on-demand, so people can revisit them whenever they need a spiritual boost, or catch up on what they missed.

"They triumphed over him by the blood of the Lamb and by the word of their testimony." — *Revelation 12:11*

Virtual Small Groups and Bible Studies

Not everyone can attend in-person Bible studies, but that doesn't mean they should miss out. Virtual small groups and Bible studies offer an excellent way to foster community and spiritual growth, even when physical gatherings aren't possible. Platforms like Zoom and Microsoft Teams make it easy to meet up, share, and learn together.

"For where two or three gather in my name, there am I with them." — *Matthew 18:20*

Make these online sessions even more engaging by incorporating multimedia resources like video clips and interactive quizzes. These tools can help deepen understanding and keep everyone actively involved.

"Let the wise listen and add to their learning, and let the discerning get guidance." — *Proverbs 1:5*

UTILIZING CHURCH MANAGEMENT SOFTWARE

Streamlining Operations

Running a church involves a lot of behind-the-scenes work, and that's where church management software comes in. Tools like Planning Center and Breeze help you manage member information, track attendance, and even coordinate volunteer schedules. This streamlining doesn't just save time—it ensures that you have accurate records and can focus more on ministry.

"Each of you should use whatever gift you have received to serve others." — 1 Peter 4:10

Planning a big event? Use these platforms to handle everything from invitations to sign-ups and reminders, making it easier for everyone to participate and stay informed.

"And let us consider how we may spur one another on toward love and good deeds." — Hebrews 10:24

Financial Management

In today's digital world, many people prefer to handle their finances online, and tithing is no different. Online giving platforms allow your members to give securely from anywhere, at any time. These tools also integrate with your church management software, making financial tracking and reporting a breeze.

"Each of you should give what you have decided in your heart to give, not reluctantly or under compulsion, for God loves a cheerful giver." — 2 Corinthians 9:7

And it's not just about collecting tithes—use budgeting software to manage church expenses and generate financial reports. Transparency in how funds are handled builds trust within the congregation and demonstrates responsible stewardship.

"The plans of the diligent lead surely to abundance, but everyone who is hasty comes only to poverty." — Proverbs 21:5

VIRTUAL COMMUNITY BUILDING

Creating Online Spaces

People crave connection, and social media offers the perfect platform for creating that sense of community. Whether it's a private Facebook group where members can share prayer requests and support each other, or a church app that provides access to sermons, event calendars, and discussion forums, these online spaces help keep your congregation engaged throughout the week.

"And let us consider how we may spur one another on toward love and good deeds." — Hebrews 10:24

Engaging Content Creation

Multimedia sermons aren't just for big churches—they're a fantastic way to make your messages more engaging and memorable. Whether it's incorporating video clips, music, or visual aids, these elements can help bring your sermons to life and make the message stick.

"The message of the cross is foolishness to those who are perishing, but to us who are being saved it is the power of God." — 1 Corinthians 1:18

Interactive Bible studies are another great way to keep people engaged. Use online tools to create quizzes, discussion prompts, and multimedia resources that make learning more dynamic and interactive.

"Your word is a lamp for my feet, a light on my path." — Psalm 119:105

CYBERSECURITY AND DATA PRIVACY

Protecting Church Information

With all this technology comes the responsibility to protect your church's information. Implementing strong cybersecurity measures—like secure passwords, encryption, and regular updates—helps safeguard sensitive data, including member information and financial records.

"Protect your heart above all else, for it is the source of life." — Proverbs 4:23

It's also crucial to be transparent with your congregation about how their information is used. Clear privacy policies build trust and ensure that everyone understands how their data is being handled.

"Above all else, guard your heart, for everything you do flows from it." — *Proverbs 4:23*

Training and Awareness

Cybersecurity isn't just for the tech team—it's everyone's responsibility. Provide training for staff and members on best practices for keeping data safe. Awareness and education are key to preventing breaches and ensuring that your church is protected.

"The wise store up knowledge, but the mouth of a fool invites ruin." — *Proverbs 10:14*

Regular audits of your digital security measures will help identify potential vulnerabilities and keep your church's information secure.

"Be diligent to present yourself approved to God, a worker who does not need to be ashamed and who correctly handles the word of truth." — *2 Timothy 2:15*

Conclusion

Embracing technology and innovation is no longer just an option for modern Christian leaders—it's a necessity. By harnessing digital communication, leveraging online worship tools, utilizing church management software, building virtual communities, and ensuring cybersecurity, churches can enhance their ministry and foster stronger connections. The key is to embrace these tools with open hearts and creative minds, ensuring that our churches thrive in this digital age while staying true to their mission and values.

XIX

What next?

As we wrap up our discussion on navigating church dynamics, it's important to take a step back and reflect on what we've learned. This chapter is about summarizing the key points we've covered, offering guidance on how to move forward, and discussing practical steps to foster unity and resolve conflicts. The journey ahead may have its challenges, but with a firm foundation of faith and grace, we can make meaningful progress.

Reflections on the Journey

Throughout our exploration, we've examined various aspects of church life, from understanding power structures to addressing conflicts and embracing transparency. Each topic has provided valuable insights into how we can build a stronger, more cohesive church community. We've learned that balancing tradition with innovation, being transparent in our operations, and fostering open communication are essential for a healthy church environment.

One major takeaway is the importance of striking the right balance. Churches thrive when they respect their traditions while also being open to new ideas that can enhance their mission. It's like managing a well-loved recipe; you keep the core ingredients but adjust the seasoning to match contemporary tastes. This balance helps ensure that our church remains relevant and effective in fulfilling its mission.

Moving Forward

Facing the challenges ahead with faith and grace is crucial. We should remember that seeking wisdom is not just a matter of strategy but also of faith. *James 1:5* offers us reassurance: *"If any of you lack wisdom, let him ask of God, that giveth to all men liberally, and upbraideth not; and it shall be given him."* This verse reminds us that we are not alone in our decision-making; we can always turn to God for guidance.

Creating a culture of openness and respect within our church is also essential. When we encourage honest communication and actively listen to one another, we build a stronger sense of community. *Proverbs 27:17* highlights the value of constructive dialogue: *"Iron sharpeneth iron; so a man sharpeneth the countenance of his friend."* Engaging in meaningful conversations helps us grow and improve as a community.

Making Necessary Changes

To address conflicts and foster unity, here are some practical steps that should be followed:

1. **Understand the Issues**: Start by identifying the root causes of conflicts and challenges within the church. Talk to members, listen to their concerns, and get a clear picture of what needs to be addressed. This helps ensure that solutions are relevant and effective.

2. **Create Clear Plans**: Once you understand the issues, develop straightforward plans to tackle them. This might involve updating policies, improving communication methods, or introducing new conflict resolution practices. Following the guidance of *Matthew 18:15-17*, which outlines a process for resolving disputes, can be helpful in addressing issues directly and respectfully.

3. **Foster Inclusivity**: Make sure that everyone feels heard and valued. Inclusivity helps prevent misunderstandings and promotes a sense of belonging. As *Galatians 3:28* tells us, *"There is neither Jew nor Greek, neither bond nor free, neither male nor female: for ye are all one in Christ Jesus."* This verse underscores the importance of unity and equality within the church.

. **Promote Accountability**: Establish clear systems for accountability to ensure transparency and trust. Regularly share financial reports, decision-making processes, and progress updates with the congregation. This openness helps prevent misunderstandings and builds confidence in church leadership.

5. **Encourage Continuous Improvement**: Adopt a mindset of ongoing improvement. Regularly review and adjust practices based on feedback and changing needs. *Philippians 3:13-14* encourages us to strive for progress: *"Forgetting those things which are behind, and reaching forth unto those things which are before, I press toward the mark for the prize of the high calling of God in Christ Jesus."* Embracing this mindset helps us continually grow and evolve.

6. **Choose Leaders Based on Merit**: One of the most significant aspects of effective church governance is ensuring that leaders are chosen based on their qualifications and character, not on personal connections or financial influence. Leadership roles should be filled by individuals who demonstrate integrity, competence, and a genuine commitment to the church's mission. *1 Timothy 3:1-13* provides clear guidance on the qualifications for church leaders, emphasizing qualities like good character, self-discipline, and a strong faith. *"A bishop then must be blameless, the husband of one wife, vigilant, sober, of good behaviour, given to hospitality, apt to teach..."* Choosing leaders based on these principles helps maintain the integrity of the church and fosters a culture of fairness and respect.

Conclusion

As we conclude this journey, let's apply the lessons we've learned with intention and care. By addressing conflicts with empathy, maintaining transparency, and balancing tradition with innovation, we can build a stronger, more unified church community. Choosing leaders based on merit, fostering inclusivity, and embracing continuous improvement are vital to our ongoing growth. Let's move forward with faith, commitment, and a dedication to serving one another in love. Together, we can navigate the challenges and create a church that reflects the best of our shared values and aspirations.

About the author

Adam K. Gondwe is a dedicated pastor, seasoned ICT professional, and author with a passion for church leadership and spiritual growth. With over a decade of experience in pastoral ministry, Adam serves as the Regional Youth Pastor at Living Waters Church International in Malawi, under the visionary leadership of Apostle Dr. S.S. Ndovie. His current book focuses on the vital aspects of church leadership, blending his deep knowledge of ministry with practical insights for modern-day pastors and church leaders.

In addition to his pastoral work, Adam is an ICT expert known for his leadership in both the spiritual and professional realms. He is also the Vice Board Chairman of Operation Mobilization Malawi (OM Malawi), an organization dedicated to transforming lives through the gospel.

Adam has written other impactful books, including *Defeating Darkness: Secrets to Spiritual Warfare* and *The Marriage Pillars: 8 Essential Tablets for Success*, reflecting his commitment to empowering individuals and strengthening their spiritual journey.

Other Books by Adam Gondwe

Defeating Darkness: The Secrets to Spiritual Warfare

This book was written with a deep desire to help and guide people through the complex and often challenging world of spiritual warfare. Today, we see an alarming rise in occult practices, witchcraft, and satanic churches across the globe, making it more important than ever to shine a light on the spiritual battles that believers face.

THE MARRIAGE PILLARS: 8 ESSENTIAL TABLETS FOR SUCCESS

Welcome to *"The Marriage Pillars: Eight Essential Tablets for Success"* in these pages, we embark on a journey of exploration into the foundations of strong and enduring marriages. This book is a collection of insights, wisdom, and practical advice gleaned from the depths of personal experience, faith, and study.

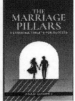

Made in the USA
Columbia, SC
26 October 2024